The Bandit Monologues

Also by Todd Carstenn

Muni Rats – Volume One
Muni Rats – Volume Two
Why I Teach

Also by G. Kent

Running with Razors and Soul:
A Handbook for Competitive Runners

Hiking in North Florida with William
Bartram: 25 Hikes – Volume One

Hiking in North Florida with William
Bartram: 25 Hikes – Volume Two

The Bandit Monologues

Todd Carstenn

G. Kent

Bandit Press

ISBN – 13: 978-1548168025
ISBN – 10: 1548168025

Bandit Press
2327 NE 8th Place
Ocala, Florida 34470
kentib@earthlink.net

This book may be ordered from the publisher, through booksellers, or online at createspace.com, amazon.com or barnesandnoble.com.

To the thousands of Lake Weir and Vanguard high school students who are members of the Carstenn - Kent family.

Contents

"If there's a book that you want to read, but it hasn't been written, then you must write it."

- Toni Morrison

Foreword

I LEARNED ALL that I knew was important in history by what hung on the walls of Gary Kent's classroom. I learned all that I know of how to deal with the problems that history presented by the contents on the walls in Todd Carstenn's classroom. The serendipitous twists and turns of events that led both of these men to inhabit teaching spaces in the same hallway of the same high school as decades of students passed through their formative years behind desks in front of them is too great a story to tell here. But I must count myself among the lucky generations to have learned much of what I carry with me today from these two.

Todd Carstenn is my dad, an English teacher, and Gary Kent, a History teacher, his best friend and colleague throughout my life. I spent countless hours from childhood through my teenage years bouncing in and out of each of their classrooms, scouring the walls for new information, or artwork, or inspiration in my own creative endeavors. They would see to it that not a bare piece of cinder block or paneling was visible. Instead, what lay staring back at the faces of the students in these rooms was proof of a reason to care about what they were being asked to grasp

The walls of Kent's room were a library of newspaper and magazine cutouts documenting the great, horrific and wonderful moments of the past hundred years in American History. The assassination of JFK in the Dallas newspaper next to a photo of Neil Armstrong walking on the moon; the fulfillment of a promise Kennedy made to the American people before his death. That juxtaposition of hope, loss and fruition in three square feet of space on what would otherwise be a blank wall, much like what was surely to be emblazoned in the minds of each student who read it. And not fifty feet away stood the doorway to Dad's room, the tie-dye colors of a homemade peace sign on white canvas shone into the hallway like a lighthouse in the dark night of adolescent torment.

While Kent's room told the tale of what happened and how to avoid repeating the mistakes and how to make sure that the things that were done right were never forgotten, Dad's room let you know it was okay to FEEL. To feel unsure, or scared, or anxious or hopeful, or really anything at all along the way. Quotes from Walden "live deep and suck out all the marrow of life" next to photos of Kurt Cobain and Jimi Hendrix; lives lived too deep possibly. But it was always part of the conversation. In his classroom that was supposed to be the house of learning about English and Literature, it became more about how to deal with the feeling his students gained when absorbing those great ideas.

The crossroads at which this book finds itself is similar to the one that is walked when going from one classroom to the next. A great moment from history or literature as it is observed by the minds of these two great educators. One tells the story of what that moment brings to mind, and lets it spark and create a new idea altogether. Spawning new characters and new universes. The other tells of feeling or memory that applies to him, but in the way of so many great writers before, applies to anyone who would read it; wrapping great personal observations into an emotional weave of universal experiences.

I learned the stories of what happened from Gary Kent. I learned to understand those stories from Todd Carstenn.

Jared Carstenn
Kailua, Hawaii

Prologue

*"What really knocks me out is a book that, when
you're all done reading it, you wish the author that
wrote it was a terrific friend of yours and you
could call him up on the phone whenever you felt
like it."*

- J.D. Salinger

HE'S A STORYTELLER. I'm essentially an essayist. Not
necessarily a partnership made in writer's heaven, but we
made it work. The it?

This book.

One night a few years ago, over beers of course, I
suggested to Gary that we write a book together. My plan
was this: we would find thoughtful and stimulating quotes
from all types of writers and thinkers, and then each of us
would respond in some way. Gary then added the idea of
the overall titles you see, like Music or God or Family and
so forth. What I thought might happen didn't happen. Since
we've been friends for thirty-five years, I'd assumed our
riffs, our "chapters" if you will, would be similar. Nope.
They are not and it's that variety that I have come to
appreciate about what The Bandit Monologues turned out
to be.

Gary is a Californian who moved east and spent
whatever time he wasn't camping in a classroom. I'm from
Wisconsin and moved south and spent whatever time I
wasn't golfing also in a classroom. His classroom was
History. Mine is English. Friends for thirty-five years, I
guess this book was an inevitability. We originally called it

The Bandit Dialogues. Bandits have some renegade in them. They come out swinging when pushed into corners. I'd like to think we did that for an entire generation of our students. As far as the "dialogue" part, the plan never was to talk TO each other, thus Bandit Monologues.

The unifying thread in each chapter, of course, is the quote or quotes. You'll see we stray far and wide from each other and even from the quote itself. But that's bound to happen when you put a California storyteller and a Wisconsin essayist together. We both love the written word; we just get to where we're going in different ways.

Here's a quote to start you on your "listening" tour of our monologues:

"A book consists of thoughts that for a moment don't mind holding hands."
> \- Garry Fitchett, *Life is a Bicycle*

Sounds about right. Enjoy.

One

Infinite

BUT I WONDER if it's that simple, Mr. Blake. Cleanse the doors of perception and *voila* – we see all? I find it neither simple nor realistic. Look, the reality is that the vast majority of us DO see all things – our lives, our kids, our jobs, our relationships – but we see all of that from behind the narrow chinks of our own caverns. We live life at the micro level. This fact is not a crushing blow. It doesn't damn us to the kind of life Henry David Thoreau brings up when he says "the mass of men lead lives of quiet desperation." I just simply and humbly believe that we, all of us, find our "infinite" in different places and different people, and it's possible that it isn't so grand and elevated as it is made to seem.

What does "infinite" mean anyway? All that is out there, all that life has to offer, the reaching of our ultimate potentials? There is a mystical sense of the word, certainly, especially for those of us who have ever listened, for example, to "The End" by big Blake fans, The Doors. Here again though, most of our lives are NOT lived that way – our infinite, our perception, or rather what we perceive through Blake's crack, is actually not infinite at all – it is real life, our real life. And most of our life is defined by very finite things like our jobs and our kids (in my case, Jared and his younger brother by two years, Dustin) and others we hold dear to our hearts.

To explain this, I have a story of when my oldest son moved out. Who knew that a single load of laundry could ever mean so much?

I was a single dad for the last few of my sons' high school years. As such it was my job to do our laundry. I wasn't great at it; no one strives to be great at laundry. I didn't separate delicates from non-delicates (Indelicates? That doesn't seem right either) . . . but that is not what this is about. At some point shortly after he graduated from high school, my son Jared told me he was moving to Hawaii. My ex-wife had moved out there and Jared came to me one day and said the equivalent of "Dad, you know I have to try this."

And I did know it. Though we didn't live on the beach in Florida, from the time the boys were small, we packed the car and headed east with body boards and skim boards. Jared's move, given these circumstances, WAS an inevitability.

I prefaced this with a reference to laundry didn't I...?

The night before Jared left, I did the laundry, and as was the usual case, I put the clothes in piles. Jared's pile. Dustin's pile. My pile. Except this time there weren't three piles. There were only two. Jared had packed for his early flight the next morning. For years I had washed clothes and there had been three piles. I looked down at Dustin's clothes, and at my clothes, and nothing else. I bawled. Unashamedly. I just let go. I would now have a son that was a ten-hour plane ride away. Another world, not my world anymore. Almost too much to take.

This wasn't my "infinite." It was my life, my son, our family, and now that family was down to two piles of laundry. That is as finite as it gets. As a literary guy, I GET symbolism. The symbolic nature of what wasn't there anymore brought me to my knees.

So, back to what started this discussion: "For man has closed himself up until he sees all things through the narrow chinks of HIS cavern." My emphasis on "his" is purposeful. That day in August of 2002, that wasn't anyone else's gut-punch, it wasn't a metaphysical void; it was mine and I felt it by observing life through the narrow chinks of MY cavern. All these years later, I simply have a son, at age thirty-two, who is much more Hawaiian than Floridian, and I am (finally) able to get a glimpse of Mr. Blake's "infinite." But it was a long time coming.

TC

I'VE NEVER BEEN sick when I took a day off from work – I always had to lie. Wouldn't it be great to be able to call in and say, "Hi, I feel great today, I'm not coming in?" Too bad that doesn't work in our society. So I'd call in using a feeble voice – cough a few times – and then run out the back door to pack up the truck.

As I pulled out of my driveway, Los Angeles was still asleep. I took the 118 east to the 210 south and exited at the

Sunland Avenue Bridge. A steep path led down to the water and entrance to Kagel Canyon. Besides my gear and usual staple of nuts, olives, cheese and chocolate bar, I brought a pint of Jack Daniel's. I planned to do some serious ruminating.

It was the first real cold day of winter. The sky appeared dark and angry, and threatened rain. I'd be fine. I had my fleece, raingear and black Navy coat. In a pocket of the coat were my ski gloves.

Kagel Canyon was extremely rugged. The trail, if that's what you wanted to call it, was rocky and difficult to follow. After hiking about five miles up the canyon, I discovered a narrow pass that led up the Little Tujunga in the direction of Mt. Gleason. Luckily, the creek was low so I was able to hop from rock to rock. I wanted to climb until there was nowhere else to go, but it was a struggle.

I pushed on.

In slow motion, an avalanche of mist poured down the Little Tujunga and swallowed the pass. Immediately it turned ten degrees colder. I clawed my way up a ravine for another twenty minutes before discovering a small chink of flat land encircled by Jeffrey pines. The aromas of vanilla and butterscotch were sweet and overwhelming. I sat on the moist grass and cracked the seal to my whiskey. The flat had an excellent vista of Mt. Baldy and was an ideal backpacking site.

I stored a mental note.

The icy air froze my face, but after a few gulps the whiskey began to work its magic. I pulled the ski gloves over my knuckles with my teeth.

I commiserated about my job. It was pure drudgery and only a means to an end. People who enjoy their jobs are the happiest and luckiest people in the world. It started to rain lightly, and then snow. I huddled under a Jeffrey pine and drank more whiskey. The snow settled in crevices and stuck to the ground. Then a blizzard arrived. I decided it would be wise to get out while I still could.

In the narrow pass, the faint trail was bordered on the right by a vertical granite wall, and on the left was a near-impenetrable stand of piñon pine. Though it was only 3:30 p.m. it was already getting dark. I had at least six miles to the Sunland Avenue Bridge. When I stopped to check my flashlight, I heard a noise and looked up. Two large gold eyes flashed from a boulder. I blinked twice to make certain they were real. It was a huge black and tan mountain lion.

This was just GREAT!

When the big cat noticed me, he crouched low on the rock and swished his long tail. I didn't budge. I couldn't remember if I was supposed to stand perfectly still or yell and throw rocks. I only knew to stand my ground.

I looked at him again and saw the infinite – the everything and everywhere – in his penetrating gold eyes.

After a moment or two, the cat appeared to relax and started to ignore me. He slipped behind a tree trunk and vanished. No way was I going to hike past that rock. I considered my options. I could attempt to scale a vertical cliff or crash into the brittle piñon pine. Son of a gun! Then I heard the creek. I knew the Little Tujunga emptied into Kagel Canyon. I draped the raingear over my head and plowed into the pines. The creek had risen to its banks from the rain, which forced me to wade up to my waist in order to follow the pass. The sodden Navy coat tried to drown me. I was freezing to death.

As I scanned the trees for the mountain lion, I discovered a switchback that led to the floor of Kagel Canyon. The rain had intensified and I needed to get out of the woods. Just as I reached Kagel Creek, I heard a soft rustling coming up from behind. It wasn't the sound of footsteps or the mountain lion. I stopped and the rustling also stopped. I listened and thought I could hear breathing. It was a breath of the infinite.

"Hello?" I yelled. No answer.

I squinted into the trees. Something was definitely following me.

I said, "You can come out now. I hear you breathing."

Nothing. The rain had stopped. The infinite appeared to be ushering me out of the canyon.

At the Sunland Avenue Bridge, a group of Chicano teens wearing red bandanas peered down at me and chuckled. One threw a rock. Another pointed. "*Mira*. It's a homeless Anglo." They all laughed it up.

"Are you sleeping under the bridge tonight?" one shouted.

I stopped and glared up at them. A devilish grin spread across my face. After experiencing the infinite in the golden eyes of a mountain lion, these dudes were punks.

"*Tu madre, hombres,*" I screeched, and waved my arms.

They looked at me again and bolted.

GK

Two

Freedom

"I felt my lungs inflate with the onrush of scenery – air, mountains, trees . . . I thought, 'This is what it means to be happy.'"
- Sylvia Plath

I HAVE BEEN an English teacher for 6,120 school days. That translates to 47,430 hours in the classroom. It is without guilt that I admit that I have found a great deal of Plath's happiness in public school classrooms for the last thirty-four years. I won't even go into the irony of Plath's death...OK...yes I will. How happy could she have been if she decided to stick her head in the oven as her final act, her last stanza as it were.

But I digress.

There are, I believe, different ways to look at what "happy" means. In Ibsen's A DOLL'S HOUSE, as she is ending her marriage to Torvald, Nora is asked, "Have you not been happy here?" Her answer is simple but revealing: "No, not happy, only merry." Without going to a dictionary, here is the difference between "merry" and "happy." "Merry" you feel from what you do. "Happy" you feel from what you are. "Merry" is surface, "happy" is soul deep. The classroom has touched my soul.

7

I was a twenty-six-year-old college dropout when I decided to get out of the bar business and try to get back into school. With no real idea what I wanted to do with my life, I found myself in Dr. Toni Lopez's 19th Century British Literature class. 19th Century British Literature was not in my wheelhouse at that time of my life, not a choice I made eagerly, but there was a spot open so I went. I have no idea what we read or discussed that first day. I also realize it would make for a better story if I did. I could explain how I well up each time I read that ode, or whatever it had been, but I simply don't remember.

Here's what I do remember: I walked into Turlington Hall that morning with no life plan; I walked out knowing I wanted to be a teacher, an English teacher. Toni made what should have been monotony into goose-bump stuff. By the way, I tell my students all the time to not use clichés, so the "goose-bump" reference seems wrong and hypocritical. But most clichés are true, and thank God this one was. But all this merely got me wanting to be a teacher, it lead me into the classroom. What has kept me here for thirty-four years? All of the following and more.

I teach English because of Winston Smith's courage in the face of the rats and the telescreen and Big Brother in 1984. I teach English because in Bradbury's FAHRENHEIT 451, a young girl motivates a fireman to tilt his head to the sky to taste the rain after a lifetime of setting fires. I teach English because I enjoy telling my kids that Osip Mandelstam's wife memorized his volumes of poetry so she could carry on his literary heritage while he was dying in a Soviet work camp. I teach English because Atticus convinced Jem that courage was not a man with a gun in his hand, but it was fighting a battle knowing it was over a hundred years before it had begun. My students never miss the courage of Maycomb, or the love or the gentleness. Atticus. Boo. Maudie. Mrs. Dubose. Tom. Scout. My sometimes-hardened teenagers, I swear, feel the same lump in their throats as I do in mine when Scout tells her dad, "Well, it would be sort of like shooting a mockingbird, wouldn't it?"

I teach English because I decided long ago poetry was not some sacred ancient relic. Poetry is a state of mind. It is not a secret rhyme scheme that only the blessed few can decipher. Poetry is your heart and your gut and it must be taken out of the parlors and put into kids' hands in classrooms, and on the street and on darkened spot-lighted cafeteria stages on Friday nights. I teach English because writing is important. In Edward Abbey's book ONE LIFE AT A TIME, PLEASE, he says, "I believe that words count, that writing matters, that poems and essays and novels – in the long run – make a difference. If they do not, then the writer's work is of no more importance than the barking of village dogs at night." The challenge of changing kids' perceptions of themselves from mere children with pencils in their hands to REAL writers is one that I confront with joy. These are not Abbey's barking dogs; these are teenagers who have ideas and perspectives that have to be heard.

I teach English because nothing on this planet, or elsewhere, is irrelevant in my classroom.

You want outer space? You have Ray Bradbury and Arthur C. Clarke. You want inner space? You have THE HOBBIT and even the Amboy Dukes singing "Journey to the Center of the Mind." You want math? Then you too can discuss the relative truth of how $2 + 2 = 5$ in Orwell's

1984. You want silly? Shel Silverstein's "Sarah Sylvia Cynthia Stout Would Not Take The Garbage Out." Sexy? Hawthorne's scarlet A. Scary? Every day's newspaper.

For thirty-four years, all of the above has been my happiness. A number of paragraphs ago, I said that it was without guilt I had found Plath's happiness not in the air, mountains or trees but in a classroom. Okay – I admit it – there is a bit of guilt. After all, the guy with whom I am writing this book has written two hiking books, and I wrote the Foreword for each of them. I GET air and mountains and trees. We have camped in the mountains where bears have wandered into our tent circle. I almost died from a cold weather overnight trip in Florida (I am not proud of that). There are sacred trees I recognize and cherish year after year on my favorite hike to a place called Pat's Island.

And yet, the classroom has been the constant thread that has been my happiness for over half my life. In fact, I realize in this entire essay, I have not used the word "job" once. Hmmm.

Toni Lopez, all those years ago, started that thread, and I am the happy result of it.

TC

TAKING OUT THE TRASH is one of the few chores I actually enjoy. I perform my duty nightly and, of course, I'm usually alone. Same was true when I lived in L.A., where hanging out in my alley was a decadent pleasure. It had 1930s-style lampposts and was lined with eucalyptus and towering black poles connected by heavy electrical wires. Garage doors and fences of wood or block, many covered with ivy, shaped the boundaries.

On this night I placed the lid back on the trashcan and gazed at the stars. Suddenly, an army of long blond-haired surfers marched down the center of the alley carrying skateboards and raving about radical tricks and gnarly speed. They headed toward Bull Creek wash off Debra Avenue. They popped cans of Coors and shouted, "Breakfast of Champions!" I joined them at a hole cut into the chain-link fence.

"What are you guys up to?" I said loudly.

They all leaped into the air.

"Dude," the leader said, "you didn't have to sneak up on us."

"Uncool, dude," another added.

I tilted my head. "You dudes must be fans of *The Big Lebowski.*"

They appeared bewildered.

"Who's the big Lebowski, dude?"

I smiled. Was that an oxymoron? "He's a cool dude, dude," I explained.

"He sounds extreme."

The night was cool and breezy. San Gabriel winds swooshed down from the Big Tujunga and ruffled our hair. A full amber moon filled the eastern sky and lit up the creek. The skaters proceeded to ride down the asphalt side of the wash, splash across a dribble of water and storm up the other side before banking and sliding back down. It was like snowboarding on a half-pipe.

"Wow!" I said. "That looks like a blast."

One of them handed me a skateboard. "Try it, dude," he said.

I hesitated. "It's been a long time."

He offered a few tips. I listened carefully, and then took off. I slid straight down, shot a rooster-tail of water into the air and zipped up the other side. Then I stepped off the board and shouted, "Yeah!"

When my instructor caught up with me, he said, "Dude, you're a natural."

"The board rides smooth."

"It's the wheels," he said. "I designed them myself."

"Can I buy it?"

"Come by my shop tomorrow on Sepulveda and Nordoff. It's called Valley Kooks, Inc. I've got a huge inventory."

"I like this one," I said.

He shook his head. "Sorry, dude, it's my favorite. But you can borrow it for the evening."

Several of the guys discussed the record for distance riding in a wash.

"It's not easy to keep going, dude," the shop owner explained. "Eventually you lose momentum. But if you can keep the sharp angles going, it's unbelievable how far you can ride." He pointed south. "Miki Dora's son rode all the way to Tarzana. He holds the record. It's gotta be at least four miles."

"Holy cow!" I'd heard surfers talk about Miki Dora at Zuma Beach. He was a legendary surfer from Malibu.

"Hey dude," one of them said. "Did you know that Edgar Rice Burroughs once lived in Tarzana?"

I grinned. "Who?"

"Burroughs, dude. He wrote the *Tarzan* series back in the 20s. Didn't you know that?"

"I thought he wrote *Naked Lunch*."

I took off on the special skateboard and quickly realized the key to long rides was to hit the water straight on. That way the moss helped you maintain speed with as little friction as possible. The ride under the full moon was exhilarating. I passed under a dozen bridges and never felt so free and happy in my life. When I reached the Tarzana city limits, I refused to cross the line. It was only fair that the distance record should stay with the son of Miki "da Cat" Dora.

GK

Three

Wanderlust

*"Wandering is the activity of the child,
the passion of the genius"*
                    - Roman Payne

*"Every dreamer knows that it is entirely
possible to be homesick for a place you've
never been to, perhaps more homesick than
for familiar ground."*
                    - Judith Thurman

WE HAVE DECIDED to call this section "Wanderlust." In my mind the "dreamer" in Thurman's quote is someone who is impacted by wanderlust. But I wonder if wanderlust is the cause or the effect. As I look back at the second half of the 1970s, the decade that really formed who I was and who I would be, it seems to have been a bit of both. Even though those years almost killed me, it makes sense at this point to explore them for a bit.

There were some moments in the 1970s that did make some sense, which maybe served as the balance for what was to come. For example, somehow, eight of my high school friends were able to talk our parents into sending us to California for our sophomore years of college. Can you imagine – eight small town Wisconsin kids ending up in

San Diego? Paradise, right? Maureen, my girlfriend, was one of the eight and I was excited for all that lay ahead. But it turned out that I was in love with the concept of California, but not California itself...and so I was the one who left. "Go west, young man." Then wander back east. Back to the University of Kentucky to begin yet another journey, this one towards becoming a college dropout.

But this essay isn't about becoming a dropout. That part of my story is boilerplate stuff. Joined a fraternity. Stayed out too late with the brothers (and the sisters when we could get them to sneak in). Stopped going to class. End of story, and the beginning of more wandering. I will admit that when I finally packed the car to leave Lexington, it was with some relief. I'd been wasting Dad's money and my time, so leaving Lexington was the sane thing to do. Where to go? My brother Jim lived in Florida and that had a nice sound to it. A Wisconsin kid who hadn't bought into California did like the sound of Gainesville. A nice sound to it? That's how I decided where to live? Jesus. So this part of my wandering was both a cause AND an effect. Cause-failed college student with no discipline. Effect-Florida here I come. But it's the next three years that I'd like to put under the microscope here. I have told this story out loud many times, but I've never written it down. I wonder why.

It seems to me that "wandering" is at least partly related to "running," running towards something or running away from it. I mean wandering does have that great tee shirt – "All who wander are not lost." The fact that I stayed with Jim for nine months rather than the two weeks I had told him I would be there, at least, retrospectively, was a clue. I needed something: family, security, consistency...all of which I had in some form, consciously or not, run from.

Then began a series of jobs that I knew in my heart were leading nowhere at all. I was a bartender at a place called Sin City (what could possibly go wrong there?). I was a bouncer at a disco club named Dub's. It was 1977; the Bee Gees and Gloria Gaynor were huge. I, however, was not huge, and as a bouncer, that was a problem.

Back to wandering.

In Robert Pirsig's *Zen and the Art of Motorcycle Maintenance*, he says near the beginning that "some channel deepening seemed to be called for." He KNEW what he needed. But at age twenty-three, introspection was not my forte. Wandering, whatever the cause, offers time for introspection, for that channel deepening. Judith Thurman's ideas about the dreamer, the wanderer as it were, being homesick for a place he's never been makes perfect sense to me as I look back. I was living an unrealistic life. Great money, free drugs, good music, days off to go to the beach or the lake, or sleep off the night before. My parents certainly didn't know what I was doing with, and to, myself. The friends I had were on the same funhouse ride that I was. Who would want that to end? I think I realize NOW that I was probably homesick for that place Thurman referenced, but again this was not the time for that introspection. I shrugged off getting fired as a not-big-enough bouncer and got a job at a rock and roll club called The Lamplighter. It was to be my last job in the bars.

Bartender, Assistant Manager, Manager. In three years I was running the place. My quick ascension, not just a mid-twenties fascination with the party life, was enough to convince me to commit myself to the bar life as a career.

Yes – this was my future. Then I got a call from the police on my night off about a shooting at The Lamplighter. And that's all it took. I had wandered for three years. Into bars at which I worked, and bars where I drank for free. I had wandered into drugs that got me high, and pills that brought me back down. The money and the lifestyle and pace of life (speed if you will...) were incredible. A single guy in a college town working at a rock and roll bar. Sign me up.

But not for me, not anymore.

So where has this gotten me?

Wandering...wanderlust...these have an almost-mythical quality to them, don't they? But my reflections here have made me aware of a few things. I have realized the difference between those two words. I had no urge to travel, to explore, to wander lustfully if you will. Everything I did was a reaction. I was living a life in which I initiated nothing. I controlled nothing, which explains the semi-destructive path I led. I was fucking lost.

So I guess what I did was simply wander. And growing older (old?) has helped me see now that my lost-ness was a product of the search itself. I had not, since childhood, been in a place in which I was comfortable, that metaphysical home. But it WAS the wandering that got me there. A whole lot closer to home than I ever imagined I could be.

TC

I FIRST HEARD about Redfern Lake from reading *Cross Creek* by Marjorie Kinnan Rawlings, but she called it by a different name. At a secluded cove on the lake was a reputedly stunning grove of old-growth cypress, many of the specimens over six hundred years old. A tiny road to the lake cut through private property and was not maintained. I needed to tread lightly. Locals who live deep inside the Ocala National Forest have a tendency to get testy with trespassers. Unfortunately, the road was nearly impossible to find and no signs pointed the way.

I drove northeast on CR 314 and stopped at Bob's Country Store in Scrambletown for beer, gas and directions. The town had earned its name during Prohibition. When government agents entered the area, all the resident moonshiners scrambled. Several short stories by Rawlings document the history and characters of the town. In the 1980s, Marion County changed the name to Cedar Creek, for obvious reasons - but there was such an outcry from locals that the county commissioners threw up their hands and re-instated Scrambletown.

I asked Bob about Redfern Lake. He scratched his belly. "You talkin' 'bout that haunted lake?"

I tilted my head. "Haunted?"

"I know where it's at, but couldn't tell you how to get there."

"What does that even mean?"

Bob grinned. "It means you should give up your dumb idea about goin' there. Folks tell me the place is real spooky."

I turned north on FR 30. After six miles I made a left at the Lake Lou turnoff. It wasn't numbered. I had been told Redfern Lake was south of Lake Lou. I tried the first road heading south, but it dead-ended at a spot where a dozen squatters had set up tents. A few of the men brandished rifles. They probably thought I worked for social services. I waved and rolled down the window.

"Do you know how to get to Redfern Lake?" I asked.

The man looked bewildered. "You talkin' 'bout that haunted lake?"

"I guess."

"I know where it's at, but couldn't tell you how to get there."

I felt like I was in an episode of the *Twilight Zone*. "Thanks anyway."

"What'd ya wanna go to that spooky lake fer?"

I backtracked to Lake Lou Road and tried the second even smaller road. When I approached a stretch of sand, I figured I was on the right track. Okay, easy does it. I slipped my Dodge Dakota into four-wheel drive and immediately got stuck. Dang! I slammed it in reverse and rocked. It didn't work. I got out and tried to dig. No good.

I started to hike out.

After about ten yards the black flies began to bite. Then two rattlesnakes blocked my way. I backed up and allowed them to slither off. At FR 30, I still had six miles to Bob's Country Store. I thought I might die of thirst. Two beat-up Chevy pickups, with shotguns and Rebel flags in their back windows, roared by in a cloud of dust. I stuck out my thumb and the second truck stopped.

"Ya mind riding in back?" the teenager asked. "I got my dogs up front."

"No problem," I said.

Scrambletown appeared to be an oasis of civilization.

"What happened to your truck?" Bob asked.

"I should have listened to you," I answered.

AAA flat refused to send anyone out into the National Forest. The lady told me that 100% of the time the caller is gone by the time the tow truck arrives.

"I promise to stay at Bob's Country Store," I said. "Do you want to talk to Bob?"

"No thank you," the lady said. "Sorry about that."

A scruffy old geezer, who looked like a cast member from the movie *The Hills Have Eyes*, plopped down a six-pack of Old Milwaukee. "What's the problem, son?" he asked.

"This is Mr. Skulls," Bob said.

I explained my predicament to Mr. Skulls. "Follow me," he said.

In the parking lot was a truck that looked like Mr. Skulls had built it himself from parts of other trucks. I noticed a big winch on the back. On the way to my Dakota, I told Mr. Skulls about my search for Redfern Lake.

He grinned. "That lake's a fairytale, son. It don' exist. You must be quite a wanderer."

Mr. Skulls yanked my truck out of the sand like it was a rubber ducky. Back at Bob's Country Store, I tried to give him twenty dollars, but he would have none of it.

"Just being neighborly," he explained, carrying his six-pack of Old Milwaukee.

"Hold on." I marched back to the freezer and picked up a case of his brand. "At least you can let me buy you a beer, Mr. Skulls," I said. "I appreciate your help."

He grinned. "Good thing you didn't find that spooky lake. You might not have made it back."

GK

Four

Family

"Now you will think of days past when you had a mother. When you are used to this horrible thing that she will forever be cast into the past, then you will gently feel her revive, returning to her place beside you."

- Marcel Proust

"It's a funny thing about mothers. Even when their own child is the most disgusting little blister you could imagine, they still think he or she is wonderful."

- Roald Dahl

MY MOM NEVER met my sons. There is no one in the world that I would rather have met her. And no one I'd rather have them meet. Sad.

And there IS a degree of sadness in this story, but it is not without a full heart. You see, my mom died of a heart attack when I was only seventeen years old. We'd had a scare a couple months earlier, in early December when she had to go to the hospital, but she made it home for what was to be her last Christmas. It was a joyous time. In mid-January, though, the heart attack took her. To say that a seventeen-year-old boy needs his mom is to say that air is important for survival. For the forty-four years she has

21

been gone, I have thought about her every day. And I do think about the fact that she never met my sons.

Mom and I were golfers in a family of tennis players. My dad and two brothers, Tec and Terry, would go to Buckner Park to play tennis. My mom and I would go to Moorland Public Golf Course to play nine holes. (Though this essay is about my mom, this is the right time to bring in a tennis-related memory. Since I didn't play tennis, I would go occasionally to watch Dad and Terry and Tec, and on these occasions I would be the water boy. I'd fill the aluminum tennis ball cans at the bubbler and take them back. There is nothing like the taste of aluminum tennis-can water. It is one of the tastes of my youth.)

Mom and I walked Moorland. No golf carts for us. We walked and talked, walked and talked, golf buddies, and dinner partners. She was this small, gentle, white-haired angel that literally everyone loved. I do have individual memories of her, one of which I will explain shortly, but what I remember most is that gentleness. Her soft voice was a sound track of my youth. I still hear it and I've tried to recreate it in my own way. My own sons, Jared and Dustin, are thoughtful and kind and they have huge hearts. And yes, I see Mom in them. Despite the fact that she missed meeting them by more than a decade.

I mentioned earlier about having a full heart. Here is a memory that simultaneously makes my heart swell and ache.

My brothers and I grew up in Wisconsin. Tec was twelve years older than I; Terry was eight years older. So by the time I was ten years old they were away at college. Not down the street at our local college. Tec was at Northwestern and Terry was at Valparaiso. To a ten-year-old boy who idolized his brothers, those colleges, though not technically far away, may have been on the other side of the planet.

I played a lot of basketball when I was young and we had a hoop secured to the top of our garage, which was about thirty yards from our back kitchen door. Even on cold winter nights, with Dad travelling and my brothers away at school, I would go out back and shoot baskets. The problem, of course, was when it got really cold the ball didn't bounce very well. And here's what Mom did.

We set up a two-ball rotation system. I would shoot outside for about fifteen minutes at which point the ball stopped bouncing because of the cold. I'd run to the back door where Mom had a warm ball waiting. The ball was warm because fifteen minutes earlier she had put it in the oven on low heat. I'd open the back screen door, toss the cold ball to her, watch her place it in the oven, grab the ball on the rug by the door, and run back to the garage for more hoops. I'd play for hours and every fifteen minutes had a new warm ball.

Two more thoughts about Mom. One specific to my brother Terry. The other, wonderfully, only mine.

If there was a rebel in our family it was Terry, the middle son. He and Dad butted heads on a number of things, but one I remember most was the length of Terry's hair. Dad was a drill sergeant, literally and figuratively. Short hair was his thing. I know, I know. This story is about my mom – I'm getting to that. Terry would leave for college in late summer and when he'd come home for Thanksgiving or Christmas, his hair would be way too long. So this is what he'd do. He'd time his arrival at home for early afternoon so Dad wasn't home yet. He'd kiss

Mom hello, and if I was home from school, me too. Then he would go get a haircut. One time he came home with long hair AND A MOTORCYCLE. We did not do motorcycles in the Carstenn family.

Dad never knew a thing about the long hair or the motorcycle. Was that deceitful of Mom? No. She was keeping the peace, because that is what she did. She was our rock, our gentle foundation. It's just what she did.

And finally, this. We grew up in a small town called Waukesha and I went to Whittier Elementary School. The name is not important. What's important about Whittier is that it was close enough for me to walk home for lunch EVERY DAY. Yes, every day from kindergarten through the end of elementary school, I walked home and ate lunch with my Mom. I'd walk in that back door, Mom would hear that wonderful screen door slam, and she'd be there with my sandwich. And we'd eat together. A seven-year lunch date. Seems like yesterday. I can still hear…well…you know.

Betty Jane Carstenn. How odd and strange life is; three of the most important people in my life never met each other. She would have loved Jared and Dustin. They would have cherished her. And all these years later, the idea that she has, as Proust's saying goes, "forever (been) cast into the past" doesn't really hurt that much anymore…because every time I think of cold nights shooting warm basketballs, walking nine holes at Moorland, Terry's hair or that motorcycle, I do "gently feel her revived," and in some way or another, return to her place beside me.

TC

I AM MY mother's son. I have her Swedish blond hair and green eyes, as well as her long legs. With those long legs, I became a high school/college cross country and track star. She was a librarian who read to me as a child and helped develop my lifelong love of books. She was also an accomplished writer who taught me the craft.

On a visit to Los Angeles, my mom and I went on a date. That's what we called it. We snuck off in my rented Jeep Wrangler and took U.S. 101 to the Malibu exit in Calabassas. Our first stops were the movie ranches at Malibu Creek State Park. The Twentieth Century lot had a grove of redwoods planted in 1910. Today they stand as the southernmost redwoods in California. It also had Century Lake where much of *Butch Cassidy and the Sundance Kid*, starring Paul Newman, Robert Redford and Katherine Ross, was filmed in 1969. The Paramount Movie Ranch was created for the TV shows *Cisco Kid* and *Zane Grey Theatre*. The well-preserved western town was most recently used to film *Dr. Quinn Medicine Woman*.

"Dr. Quinn was my favorite show," Mom said.

I smiled. "I liked Jane Seymour."

Next we pulled off on the south side of the Malibu Tunnel to gawk at the outline of the infamous nude pink lady. Her busty outline was still visible on the rocks high above the tunnel. A certain artist sure had some guts to climb up there.

We zipped up the Pacific Coast Highway, or PCH, and stopped at Howe's Market in Trancas for a bottle of wine. In the liquor aisle, I selected a bottle of La Crema chardonnay. At that moment, the building shook and customers in other aisles screamed. It was a mild California earthquake. Mom grabbed my sleeve as bottles fell from the shelves and shattered on the tile floor. It smelled like a winery. When the rumbling stopped, I noticed I held the last intact bottle of La Crema.

"Lucky," I said. Mom burst out laughing.

At Zuma Beach we waded into the surf and watched the surfers carve up the six-foot swells. They were spectacular. To the south was the pinnacle where Charlton Heston discovered the Statue of Liberty buried in the sand in the film *Planet of the Apes.* Mom and I scaled its bluff and enjoyed views of Point Dume Beach, Santa Catalina Island and a pod of migrating whales.

We drove back to Malibu for an early dinner at Moonshadows Restaurant. They had valet parking.

"How much do you tip a valet guy?" I asked.

Mom said, "He should be happy with a couple of bucks."

In the lobby, I asked the hostess the same question.

"When it rains," she said, "I give him a couple of bucks to bring my car up front."

Our waitress arrived and brought more chardonnay. "You're sitting at the table where Mel Gibson ate last night," she chirped. "He later got arrested on the PCH."

The view and blackened mahi-mahi made a perfect end to our date. When the valet guy handed me the keys to the Jeep, I opened my wallet and saw that I had no ones. Dang! I handed him a fiver and he was VERY happy.

That day was the last time I saw my mom. She passed away two weeks later. When I heard the news, in Florida, I sat in a darkened room with a box of tissues and tried to remind myself that I'd always be my mother's son.

GK

Five

Sports

*"Every champion was a contender
that refused to give up."*
— Rocky Balboa

*"Remember that guy who gave up?
Neither does anybody else."*
— Anonymous

THOSE WHO CAN, DO. Those who can't teach…or coach.

I had always considered myself an academic, maybe even a bit of an intellectual. English degree. Master's Degree in English Education. Lucky enough to teach young people in elite Advanced Placement and International Baccalaureate programs. I even teach a class called Theory of Knowledge. High level stuff, right? But this also might explain my conflicted reaction when, for the last thirty years, a certain group of kids calls me "Coach."

For twenty-three of my thirty-four years of teaching I have coached: fifteen years as a tennis coach and eight years as a golf coach. Additionally, when my sons got old enough to play Little League, I coached them too. But more of that later.

The fact that I coached minor sports, non-revenue-producing sport, is probably important because I was under

27

no pressure to win. No athletic director ever came to me saying, "Sorry, Todd, I think we need to take this golf program in a different direction." My point is that this allowed me to love the kids I coached as much as the actual sport. I was and am a lifelong golfer and tennis player, and I simply wanted my players to love those games, get as much joy out of them, as I did. And in my mind that had absolutely zero to do with winning and losing, which ultimately let me be myself. So it's an odd thing, isn't it...that I clearly loved the coaching part of coaching, but was ambivalent about being called "Coach." Maybe it was the concern that I'd be labeled merely a coach, and I realize now that even that statement sounds elitist and superior. But there are a few meaningful but simple examples of what being called "Coach" means to me, and each one of them, in hindsight, scrapes away at those conflicted feelings.

One of these moments happened four of five years ago when I was at the golf course. A thirty-something guy comes up to me and says, "Hey Coach." I was actually the one who needed coaching this time, on names, because it had clearly been many years since I had seen him. But this kid, this man, turned out to be Ross Jones, who I had coached in Little League with my boys, twenty-five years earlier. He had gone away to college, married and had come back home to start a family. And part of this "home" he had returned to, a small part but certainly still a part, was an older guy who used to lob balls to him at batting practice and correct his posture while fielding ground balls all those summers ago. To Ross, I was "Coach." And it will always be so. Interesting.

I don't coach teams anymore, I do my own thing teaching private tennis lessons around town. One of my players, who actually happens to be a student in my English class at the moment, is a girl named Taylor. I met her when she was a 9th grader; now she is a senior. She is a good solid high school tennis player, but more importantly she is a world class young lady. Along the way, since we started lessons a few years ago, Taylor has had some heart trouble, so we've had to adjust the workouts and adapt the lessons. I have not wanted her to overdo it. She wears a heart monitor that intimidates me much more than it seems to bother her. As we were leaving for Christmas vacation a few weeks ago, she came up after class and gave me a hug and a present. This is what she wrote on the box of chocolates: "Thanks Coach. Thanks for everything." I am her teacher in two high-level classes in an International Baccalaureate curriculum, but she calls me "Coach." I knew the minute I read the "Thanks for everything" part of the note that it had nothing to do with tennis. She knew I cared about her whether she had a tennis racket in her hand or not. That's what "Coach" means to her and it is what it has come to mean to me.

I mentioned earlier that I coached my sons in Little League Baseball. I also coached my oldest son Jared when he played varsity high school tennis. With his mom and me separated, I thought spending time with him on the court would make sense. The boys did live with me, but I still thought simply being around him would be a positive. And at times, it was. The obvious implication of that last brief sentence was that there were many times it was not, and way too many times it was just plain awful. But we did make it through, as you'll see.

Not to get too deep in the weeds with tennis strategy, but my style of play and the style I've always tried to get my players to buy into, is to keep the ball in play, be patient, and wait for the opponent to make a mistake. That didn't work with Jared. He often told me he'd rather lose going for big flashy winners than win by merely keeping the ball in play. That conflict lasted all four years and made me certain I had turned a game that I loved into a game that he hated.

But then there's this. Jared is now a tennis pro in Kailua, Hawaii, and we talk tennis ALL THE TIME. He loves the game as much as I ever did. He has been a tennis pro, a tennis COACH for over ten years. I have watched him give lessons. I have seen his patience with his juniors. I have heard his players, young and old, call him "Coach Jared." You can't make that up. "Coach Jared." Life is good.

I'll end with this.

How do we measure the relative success of what we do? How can we quantify the results of simple human interaction? I guess getting a call from a former player asking my wife and me to be his sponsors at his baptism might qualify as success. I met Steve when he was a fourteen-year-old freshman trying out for golf. I had no idea of the role I would play in his life over the next eight or nine years. But that's really it, isn't it...we can't know the role we'll play in someone's life when we first meet them. Along the way, through his high school years we spent hundreds of hours on the golf course together and it didn't take all that long for me to find out I needed to be more than a coach to Steve. I remember his midnight call, tearful and sobbing, telling me of his dad's DUI arrest.

How hard it had been for Steve to find any respect for that kind of behavior. Here's a sixteen-year-old seeing his dad at his lowest. I was able to help him pick up the pieces of that night. But I admit that was a tough night, and it made for an uncomfortable moment when I saw his dad the next afternoon when he picked up Steve from practice.

That his parents' marriage ultimately fell apart was not a huge surprise. And I guess me taking a greater role in his life wasn't a surprise either. What was heartening though, was the baptism thing. All these years later, no longer a squirrelly, gangly fourteen-year-old, but now a twenty-three-year-old college senior, he had made a grownup decision: he had asked me to be by his side as he became an official child of God. Was I a coach? A dad? A mentor? Yes. Yes. And yes.

How do we measure the relative success of what we do? How can we quantify the results of simple human interaction? As I now look back at my conflicted attitude about being called a coach, I will think of Steve, and Ross and Taylor and my own Jared, and I will have my answer.

TC

MY PARENTS WERE traveling to Europe for ten days, so my wife Elaine and I flew out to Los Angeles in order to house sit…actually our main responsibility was to keep the dog company. My dad loved his cocker spaniel more than he loved my two brothers and me combined.

On our second day in the Valley, we drove the folks to LAX for their international flight. The airport was its usual

31

bedlam. LAX makes Atlanta and O'Hare seem like Buddhist temples, plus the place is always under some type of construction, which adds to the chaos. It was 3:45 p.m. when we dropped them off – just early enough to beat the rush hour traffic on our return to Granada Hills.

NOT!

As we drove up the ramp to the 405, we were greeted by the kind of six-lane bumper-to-bumper traffic that causes a variety of mental disorders that would require years of therapy at an institution in Austria in order to recover. The Santa Monica Boulevard exit was in one-half mile. Twenty minutes later, it was one-quarter mile.

I had to pee. How do people in L.A. make it home every day without needing to use the facilities? I pictured scores of drivers leaping out of their cars so they could pee on the asphalt. The poor ladies!

I exited onto Wilshire with the idea of taking Old Sepulveda Pass over the hill. No possible way the pass could be worse than the freeway. The off-ramp was four lanes. I seemed to recall Sepulveda Pass was to the east, but after pulling into the right lane I saw a sign that pointed left.

"The gods are toying with me," I said.

"I have to pee," Elaine exclaimed.

Every light at the intersection was red. No cars were moving. I felt like I was in *Seinfeld's* bizarro world. I made a snap decision to run the light and turn left, cutting off three lanes of traffic. "I'm from Florida," I would whine to the police. "I freaked out."

I made it!

Old Sepulveda was as clogged as the freeway. At Mulholland Drive, I got back on the 405 and inched down the hill to the Ventura Freeway where the traffic finally opened up. What should have been a thirty-minute drive turned into a three-hour tribulation.

I slammed the front door to my parents' house and vowed never to get on a freeway again until we left L.A.

"I hate this zoo," I ranted.

Elaine didn't grow up in L.A. "I thought it was exciting," she said.

"Mark my words," I thundered. "Never again."

Someone knocked on the door. It was 6:50 p.m.

A neighbor smiled at me. "Hello, remember me?"

"Of course," I said. "Please come in."

"I have two tickets to the Dodgers game tonight and can't use them. Would you be interested? The game starts at 7:30. I came over earlier, but you weren't home."

Ten minutes later, we were driving south on the Golden State Freeway heading for Dodger Stadium.

"You just swore you wouldn't drive on a freeway for the rest of our visit," Elaine said.

I was aghast. "Are you joking? It's the Dodgers."

"So what? Baseball is boring."

Jackie and Pee Wee Reese. Duke, Gil, Sandy and Drysdale. Garvey, Dusty, Lopes, Russell and the Penguin. Fernando and Orel. A Detroit Tiger turned Dodger legend – Kirk Gibson. I bleed Dodger Blue!

Chavez Ravine was spectacular at any time of the year, but no more so than under the lights. It sparkled like the Pacific Ocean. The air turned crisp and was filled with the aroma of peanuts and Dodger Dogs. Our seats were in the 11th row behind the Dodgers' dugout.

"Wow!" I said.

"Isn't it better to be behind home plate?" Elaine asked.

A big handsome rookie catcher named Mike Piazza stood in the on-deck circle. He swung his bat and grinned at the crowd. People in our section were yelling, "Mike. Hey, Mike." I swear he made eye contact with me and nodded.

It wasn't a good day for Piazza. He went 0-4 with two strikeouts and a couple of fly balls. In the top of the ninth, the Dodgers were up by one run. There were two outs with a man on second. The batter lashed a sharp single to right field and the man on second was waved home by the third base coach. Right fielder Raul Mondesi fired a line drive home.

The big handsome rookie catcher Mike Piazza caught the ball on one hop, blocked the plate and applied the tag. Out! Game over – Dodgers win. It's the most exciting play in baseball. The stadium erupted with cheers.

Last week, twenty-one years later, the big handsome catcher Mike Piazza was inducted into baseball's Hall of Fame.

GK

Six

Wild

*"Grant me some wild expressions, Heavens,
or I shall burst."*
            - George Farquhar

*"To run with the wolf was to run in the shadows,
the dark ray of life, survival and instinct. A
fierceness that was both proud and lonely, a
tearing, a howling, a hunger and a thirst."*
                - O. R. Melling

*"Hidden in the glorious wildness
like unmined gold."*
                - John Muir

MARSHALL SWAMP. Barr Hammock Preservation Area. The La Chua Trail in Paynes Prairie State Preserve. Carney Island Recreation and Conservation Area. The Sand Hill Sinkhole Trail in Silver River State Park. These places are music to a hiker's ears. Swamp. Preservation. Preserve. Conservation. Trail. Park. These words are sustenance for a hiker's soul.

I consider myself a hiker. Not an "Of course I've done the Appalachian Trail" hiker. Not a Continental Divide hiker. Not even a Pacific Coast Trail hiker. But a hiker nevertheless. To that end, this year I named my spring break vacation, "Five Hikes in Five Days." I came up with the name the week before and it thus obligated me to do it. What a great five days it was... "unmined gold" indeed.

There is a difference between "the wild" and "wilderness." I live in Central Florida, so calling it "the wild" would make me a peddler of hyperbole. But "wilderness"? Oh yes. There were times that even though I knew State Road 35 was less than a mile away, I heard no cars and saw no people. Sometimes the illusion of remoteness feels as genuine as the real thing. On that first trip on the Marshall Swamp Trail, I had forgotten my camera but I did have my phone. I also took a thirty-second video and sent it to my wife. After I sent it, I sat on a downed tree because I wanted to see it. And this is what struck me – not what it looked like but what it sounded like. Bird calls were the sound track to my day. I guess I had hiked for long enough for their songs to become a bit like white noise. I felt a bit guilty at that. Birds sing because they can (sort of like children dance before they know there's music) and I had missed it. That will not happen again.

I mentioned my camera earlier. For the next four hikes I brought it. Lens cap off. Hanging around my neck. Ready to go. Photography attempts the impossible; it tries to capture moments. But part of the wonder of particular moments is that they are just that – frozen time. But time never stops and I believe that is why when we look at the pictures of those captured moments we sometimes feel defeated, we feel cheated, because what we saw the moment we clicked our camera button...that is not what appears on the screen or the four by six inch photo. I'll never forget when I hiked to the "Secret Falls" just outside of Honolulu and when I saw the pictures afterward, I was near tears. That is not what I SAW. And yet it was. Maybe it's all part of the idea of wilderness or being tamed.

Knowing all that, I am still glad I had decided to bring my camera from there on out. The next day, at the trailhead, The La Chua trail had four or five warning signs: gators, bison, venomous snakes. The usual. My favorite one though was one that was bright yellow with big black block letters that read "USE EXTREME CAUTION. REMEMBER THIS IS NOT A ZOO OR A THEME PARK." Hilarious. A wilderness area in Florida surrounded by marsh and swamp and yet some Griswold needs to be reminded that this isn't Disney. The Disneyfication of Florida is to blame for a sign like that even being necessary. Thankfully, most attraction-goers stay away from places where they can't conveniently get a sno-cone.

And the days flew by. In the car at 7:30, at a trailhead by 8. Spring in Florida is still cool, so forty to fifty degree morning temps were the norm, and were welcomed. My third hike, the Silver River State Park, was the most basic of them all and yet still held so much beauty. If you're around it enough, even the Florida Scrub becomes enchanting. Dry, sandy trails. Breezes soughing through the pines. Miles of it. The symmetry of looking past and through acres of tall straight lines, the pine trees as majestic in their straightness as any haunting moss-covered oak. The highlight was the sinkhole. I made my way down to the bottom of it and saw the rooted up ground. Wild boars are common in these parts and these were fresh marks. I stepped lightly, listened intently, and didn't stay down in that sink for long. Wild boars aren't necessarily your friend when they are surprised.

After each hike, I immediately uploaded my pictures and had the best of them printed. I know, waiting until the week was over would have made more sense, but the pictures, each late afternoon, were a reminder that I had done something special that day, that I had been an active participant in the powerful play that goes on around us constantly, and that I was contributing my verse. (My hat is off to Walt Whitman for this last idea).

Day four then, was the Fox Trot Loop Trail at Carney Island Park, and the turkey were the absolute stars of the show that day. It was mating season, so I was told, and I came upon three or for rafters (the turkey aficionado's word for "Flock"), and the males were in full strut, fanned out as it were; clearly they were proud of themselves. I kept my distance, lens zoomed in, because I did not want to interrupt this part of nature's dance. Eventually they waddled off into the brush and I went on my way.

I mentioned before that sometimes we are disappointed by the pictures we take. That afternoon, however, was golden. The fanned-out plumes were much larger and grander than I had thought, seeing them only through a narrow lens. It adds to my belief that the wilderness can surprise us in so many ways. I begin each hike with an open mind. I say, "OK, here I am. What do you have for me today?" And there is always an answer. Always. Isn't that something...

Finally, like starting to read the last book of my favorite author (I'm looking at you, Ray Bradbury), I approached my last hike of the week with a tinge of sadness. As much as I was looking forward to driving north a bit to Barr Hammock Preserve, this was to be my last hike in a glorious week of hikes.

This hike though turned out to be a bike ride. Barr Hammock is a seven-mile trip with four straight-line berms all surrounded by marsh and swamp and wetlands and prairies. The signs warn me to stay on top, on the levee. It doesn't take long for me to be reminded that I am not alone. Hawks abound.

One in particular was actually the stuff of nightmare. I stopped riding frequently, and got off the bike to look around. Almost by accident I saw him. His eyes and part of his long wide nose were all that was visible peeking out of the reeds and water. Those eyes didn't blink. He was as still as still could be. There was a prehistoric otherness to him. We didn't mind-meld, I didn't "become" him, but there ARE moments when we are out in the wild that simply cannot be duplicated anywhere else. My zoom lens allowed close access. Close enough anyway. I will never forget that creature.

Then my trip ended, my fifth hike in five days, done. Bike on the bike rack and I headed home.

I often wonder what the difference is, between a photographer and just a guy with a camera in his hand. I also wonder when photography becomes art. I don't know if this is an answer but when I'm "out there" I feel like a real photographer and that the result is real art. It isn't me, though; it is what I see before me. Our good friend Edward Abbey said, "A man on foot or horseback, or on a bicycle, will see more, feel more, enjoy more in one mile than the motorized tourist can in a hundred miles." And that's just it isn't it? Every mile matters. Every path. Every sinkhole.

Marsh. Lake. Preserve. Prairie. Hammock. Stream. Every forest pond. They all matter.

I'll end with this. When I hear of the child who now holds sway in the White House, the people's house, when I hear that he wants to roll back environmental protections, when I learn of the draconian mindset that he and his cabal have toward all wilderness that we hold sacred, I cringe. But then I think of my long-nosed friend, the alligator, and his prehistoric otherness and realize he and his ilk have pre-dated us and will outlive even the most shortsighted tweeters imaginable, by millions of years. Finally, I realize there are so many more trails to be discovered, not new ones necessarily, but new to me.

Five Hikes in Five Days. A five-day re-awakening of my wilderness soul. Life is good.

TC

I SAT AT THE BAR in the Cowboy Saloon on the square in Jackson, Wyoming. The bar stools were actually horse saddles. Earlier in the day I had hiked an obscure trail along Granite Creek in Grand Teton National Park and met only eight hikers on the trail – that is the equivalent of encountering only eight people in Times Square.

I was drinking Sierra Nevada pale ale. Two National Park rangers were seated in the saddles next to me. In the corner of the bar was a stuffed wolf. I turned to the rangers and said, "Guess that poor guy wandered a little too far south."

Neither ranger smiled. The female glared at me.

"That's how most of the Yellowstone wolves die," she growled. "The moment they wander out of the park, they're fair game for any hunter or rancher."

"I thought they were protected," I said.

"Only in the park."

"Too bad they can't read a park map."

She proceeded to give me a history lesson. After a shameful legacy of slaughter and woeful protection laws, gray wolves were reintroduced into Yellowstone's Lamar Valley in 1995. Famed conservationist Aldo Leopold had suggested stocking Yellowstone with wolves back in 1944. He argued the wolves would restore the ecological balance among elk, deer and coyote. The Sierra Club was initially against the plan because it lacked enforcement outside of the park, but threw in its support when a fund was established to reimburse ranchers for loss of livestock so they wouldn't have a reason to kill rogue wolves. However, as the number of wolves went up, the U.S. Fish and Wildlife Service removed the wolf from the endangered species list in 2008, and Montana hunters killed a large number of wolves known to frequent the northeast section of the National Park.

"The wolves are battling for their existence," the male ranger said. "Ranchers perpetuate the myth that wolves are dangerous to people, but there has not been one wolf attack on a human being in the history of Yellowstone National Park."

"I wanna see a wolf," I exclaimed. John Muir said wolves were "hidden in the glorious wilderness like unmined gold."

The female said, "The Lamar Valley is home to ten packs of six or seven wolves. Most are collared."

"What's my chance of spotting one?"

"Look for the wolf people," the male ranger said.

"The who?" I imagined a group of half-human, half-wolf mutants roaming the canyons.

"The people who study the wolves," he said. "You'll know 'em when you see 'em."

I bought the second round.

The rangers said early morning or evening were the best times to see a wolf. I left my motel room at 4:00 a.m. It was a two-hour drive to Lamar Valley. Luckily, it was too early in the morning to be trapped by a bear or bison traffic jam.

"You're an early bird," the ranger at the tollbooth said.

"I wanna see a wolf," I said.

"Look for the wolf people."

Lamar Valley, of course, was beyond description. The river wound lazily along the south side of the road, lined with scattered lodgepole pine. I turned into a small parking lot at the turnoff to Island Lake. Three white vans were parked in a row. I looked up at a small knoll and saw a dozen people wearing headphones and manning fancy equipment.

Holy cow! The wolf people!!

No one noticed when I reached the top.

"What are you guys doing?" I asked loudly.

They all jumped.

"Jesus," one said, "you didn't have to sneak up on us."

I apologized.

One of the girls said, "Be real quiet. Lamar Valley pack number four is just behind those trees. They cross the highway each morning on their way to the Lamar River."

I peered into one of the telescopes. "When can we see them?" I whispered.

"Soon."

I noticed two ranger trucks down by the parking lot with their red lights flashing. I said, "I wonder what those guys are doing?"

"Looks like they're writing a citation."

I looked closer. Crap! It had to be me. I was parked in the first space. "I may have parked in a handicapped spot."

I raced down the slope.

"I'm sorry, guys," I yelled. "I'll move it immediately."

The rangers appeared confused.

"What are you talking about?" one asked.

I pointed. "Aren't I parked in a handicapped zone?"

They looked. "No, you're fine."

"Then why do you have your lights flashing?"

"We want people to slow down," the other one said. "Wolf pack number four should be crossing the highway at any moment."

I trudged back up the hill.

"Sorry," the first girl said. "You missed the wolves."

"What?"

"They ran across the meadow and headed for Island Lake."

I hung my head. "Marvelous."

GK

Seven

Surrender

"You are only a prisoner when you surrender."
        - Tad Williams

"Surrender to events with hope."
        - Alain de Botton

*"The greatness of the man's power is
the measure of his surrender."*
        - William Booth

"WE REGRET TO inform you that we are unable to publish your manuscript." Ouch. I have been writing and sending off articles for the better part of thirty years. Time does NOT heal all wounds, contrary to the old adage. Writing for publication is a daunting task, and even big-time writers (don't look for our names on that list...yet) get their share of rejection. But being a writer is a lesson in hope. The easy route IS to surrender to the frustration, to the seeming unfairness of the whole publishing business. But there is always one more article to write and send away. Hope simply has to be in the heart of every writer. Whenever I go to my mailbox and retrieve an envelope with the name of a magazine to which I've sent an article, my pulse quickens. The suspense though, mercifully, is over quickly. The formula is like this: thick envelope = bad

44

news. The envelope is thick because they have sent my article back along with their "We regret to inform you" sentiments. The other part of the formula: thin envelope = a possibility of acceptance because they have not sent my article back. This certainly is not a foolproof method, but it has been painfully accurate for me.

Every semester I read selected rejection letters I've accumulated over the years to my students. The topics for my writings, I tell them, are these: my family and my teaching. I have two sons and I have written articles (all returned) for magazines such as *Today's Christian, Parent, Parenting,* and *Readers Digest.* Proudly I have written about Little League baseball and seeing my sons grow up. No go on those. I am a teacher. That's what I am. As a result, I have sent countless articles and scores of my wonderful (I know they're wonderful; just ask me) teaching ideas to magazines famous and obscure. From *English Journal* to *Instructor Magazine,* I have collected rejection letters. I have even tried my hand at writing the text for a unique Christmas card, which I sent to Gibson Greeting Card Company. Same result. These rejection letters, I tell my kids, are my C's, D's, and F's. Why do I do it? Why admit, indeed publicize, my failures? Because every day I get to see and participate in THEIR C's, D's, and F's. Why shouldn't they be allowed to participate in mine? We writing teachers are forever preaching to our neophytes that they can learn from the comments in margins we offer on each returned assignment. For years I have been telling my students, "You can learn as much from getting a paper back as you did from writing it the first time." I try to show them that I learn from these rejections like I hope they learn from what I have put on their papers.

The day I read them the letters proceeds something like this. The timing of reading my rejections to them is crucial. I wait until after I've passed back a paper which was either particularly difficult or on which their grades were poor. When I pass papers back I have my kids write what I call "Comments On Comments" which forces them to paraphrase positive (but constructively critical) responses I have made on their papers. After "Comments On Comments" I tell them to put their journals away and get comfortable. Not overly dramatic, but not without a bit of theater, I reach into my desk and grab a stack of what to them must appear like nice stationary. This stack, envelopes included, I drop (PLOP) on a student desk which I sit on when I talk to them.

Then I begin. I explain that I am a writer, in addition to being a teacher. By this time each semester my students know me well enough to know that the written word is one of my passions. That statement, that I'm a writer, does not come as any great shock. After all, I have been writing with them every day since the beginning of school. I proceed to explain though, the process of sending articles to magazines and my primary topics for those articles. I conclude this initial introduction with the first mention of the "R" word: rejection. At this point I simply tell them I want to read some of these letters to them. No preaching (yet) about "See how I learn from my mistakes." Too early for that. I pick a letter from the pile and start to read. The first one might be from *Instructor Magazine.* I sent them what I thought were innovative methods with which to teach John Steinbeck's novella THE PEARL. I read most of the letter to them but repeat the most important line: "The editors on our manuscript review committee have given it a careful reading, and we regret that we are unable to publish it." Of course my students will catch the recurring theme of "regret" before long. I do add though, that the letter itself appears to have been signed by a real person, because it looks like real blue ink above the stamp of the editor's name. When you have read as many "No thank you's" as I have, the fact that a real person took the time to sign it, well, let's just say that feels like a moral victory.

I move on. I tell my kids that I sent this same article, which I called "Kino's Lessons Learned By Schools," to another magazine called *Contemporary Education*. Geez, my article is about how modern (dare I say "contemporary") schools might learn from the lead character's mistakes in this book. I was sure I had found the right place, a magazine which would appreciate a teacher relating classic literature to today's classroom... "We regret to inform you that your manuscript does not meet our editorial needs." After reading this to my students, I look up and say, "Sorry? THEY'RE sorry?" I show them the letter which is a one-sentence rejection on a legal-sized piece of paper and they see that the magazine editors did not bother with small talk to make me feel better about my writing.

The next letter I read to them is from *Parenting Magazine*. It is addressed to "Dear Contributor" and signed by a stamped "Sincerely, The Editors." I joke with my students that how sincere can they be if they wouldn't even sign their names. *Parenting*'s rejection letter took the form of a checklist. "We are unable to use your submission for the following reason(s)." Five or six were not checked before I came to the one that was. The one reason which made their magazine unable to use my article was this: "The article style does not suit our needs." I repeat that line for my kids. "The article's style does not suit our needs."

As I said before, I do not get overly dramatic reading my rejections, but I do attempt to make the kids feel what I felt upon receiving them. I tell them this: my guess is that if you want to insult a writer, you tell him his "style" doesn't work. I tell my students, who are now genuinely interested in what we are doing, that this particular letter from *Parenting,* hurt me the most because it said they did not like my style. My style is my writer's DNA, it is my thumbprint, and it was found wanting. Every student at some point has been told that WHAT they were writing was alright, but THE WAY in which they wrote it was not. They too have been told that their style didn't fit. As a result, it is usually when I read this *Parenting* letter that my students officially begin to understand why I'm doing this.

I move on, but some students are getting antsy. Geez, Mr. C, haven't you EVER gotten ANYTHING published? I tell them to be patient as I open the next envelope.

One funny aspect about this entire process is my kids begin to listen for the telltale "We are sorry…" or "We regret to inform you…" With each new letter I read, they share my pain, in a humorous oh-no-not-again sort of way. They also, because I make a big deal out of it, pay close attention to whom the letter is addressed, whether it's addressed to "Dear Contributor" or "Dear Mr. Carstenn." In addition, I mention my awareness of the closing: is the letter signed by a real air-breathing human in real blue ink or is it stamped on the anonymous literary assembly line?

My purpose in stressing these seeming trivialities is to try to make them walk in my shoes a bit, to feel slighted when no one saw fit to make it appear that some sincere thought went into the rejection of my work.

This leads me to the funniest rejection letter I ever received. I wrote an article about being a young dad of growing boys and sent it to a small magazine called *Today's Christian Parent.* On occasion, I do become desperate. In my mind, a small magazine based in Cincinnati would be more likely to accept my work than one published on Fifth Avenue in New York City. I tell my students, as rationale for offering my work to *Today's Christian Parent,* that I am a good dad, a good person. I'm certainly no axe murderer, so this magazine seemed right for me. I open the letter.

"Dear Contributor." Of course this is not a good sign. Next I tell my kids to listen very carefully to the first word of this letter. And then I continue with that first word. "Sadly..." I swear on a stack of First Edition Warriner's Grammar books, the first word in this letter is "Sadly." Well my students DO see the humor here, so I have to settle them down before I continue. "Sadly, *Today's Christian Parent* will no longer be published." Amid the laughter, I say, "Yep, I sent my article to a magazine that went out of business." I know they aren't laughing at me, because I'm laughing at the irony of it too.

Now though, it's time to get to the point. I now retrieve from the stack of my rejections, the one from *English Journal.* I make sure all my students know that it is an English teacher's Bible; it is the *Sports Illustrated* of magazines for us. I also tell them that once in a while we all do things even though we know we'll fail. Atticus Finch defended Tom Robinson though he knew he was defeated one hundred years before he began. And I, rejection letter Collector Extraordinaire, tried to get published in our Bible, the *English Journal.*

They know what's coming, but I read it anyway. "Dear Mr. Carstenn, I regret to inform you..." The piece I had chosen to send was one of the best I'd ever written. The article was an explanation of a unit I had done on some short stories, and the incredible and surprising impact it had on my students. When I write, I can FEEL whether or not it is my best, and whether or not it might be publishable. This article was THAT good. And they had turned me down. But now I tell my students, "I'm getting close to making my point."

Near the end of this three paragraph letter, which appears to be signed personally by Ben Nelms, the editor, is this statement: "We hope this response does not discourage your submission of future manuscripts to us." I repeat this and tell my kids to remember it. Meanwhile, to assuage some of their concerns that I must be a loser to accumulate so many "We regret to inform you" notes, I read with a flourish, of course, my first two acceptance letters. The first one was from *Teacher Magazine* and the other was from *Writing Teacher Magazine.* When I read the acceptance from *Writing Teacher,* we all laugh loudly because the editor had addressed the letter to "Todd Carlston." I tell them I could not have cared less that she spelled my name wrong because I had finally been accepted. Somewhere. By Somebody. In occasional classes I've had students applaud when I read, "We think your piece would work well." I actually believe they feel, by this time, that they were involved in the writing process with me.

Finally I open one last envelope. As I just mentioned, I had told them how much the article I had sent to the *English Journal* had meant to me. I also told, actually admitted, it is sometimes a bit risky to get too emotionally attached to what they write because it is easy to get hurt by the response they might receive. After all, writers write what is in their hearts and when someone says, "I regret to inform you," or worse yet, when a teacher chisels a C or D or F on their paper, it does hurt. So the kids knew how attached I was to this particular article.

So attached was I, I go on, that I would not accept their initial "No" as an answer, not even from the *English Journal.* I decided to revise my original article, to re-work it to make it better, more publishable. My students know in my class that the word "revise" means what its Latin root meant it to mean: "To see again." Too many students think revise means "to copy over and make the teacher think I changed a few words." Ha! Since I believe in the revision process so strongly, I looked at my article again, and changed some ideas, added more effective language, and resubmitted it. Just like the puny 1980 United States Olympic Hockey team took the ice against the mighty Russians, I was once again taking on the mighty *English Journal.*

I take the letter from its envelope, and I think my kids sense what will come next. "Dear Mr. Carstenn, I am happy to inform you..." and the kids can't hear the rest because they are cheering. They're cheering a letter. A simple letter. And maybe, just maybe, they're cheering me for hanging in there. Once I quiet the masses, I begin to make my last point of the day. From the original *English Journal* rejection letter, I repeat the words I told them to remember: "We hope that this response does not discourage your submission of future manuscripts to us."

Rejection is painful, whether that rejection takes the appearance of a "No thank you" from a magazine or a grade a student receives on a writing assignment. My point is, I hope the MY responses to THEIR submission will not discourage them in their future work for me. The connection, finally, has been made. We, all of us, are writers. Our assignments might differ, as well as the way in which we are notified of our success or failure. Nevertheless, we are on the same team. We are writers.

For the rest of the year, I keep my students informed on the articles I have sent away and any new rejections or acceptances. I don't continue to do this because I feel like I have to; I do it because they are now a part of my team.

TC

MY UNCLE DWIGHT gave me a vintage map of Kings Canyon National Park from 1954. When comparing it to newer maps, I discovered a spur trail off the Redwood Creek Loop that was not included on the newer maps. This lost trail intrigued me. It was a trail that no longer existed. If you are a trail that no longer exists in the backcountry of a National Park, you are about as lost as it gets.

I asked a ranger about the trail. He informed me that discontinued trails are returned to their natural state. However, many of the older trails were marked with orange tin squares nailed to the trees. "Although the trail is gone," he said, "if you can locate the orange tin squares you might be able to hike the lost trail."

I studied the 1954 map. Two tributaries flowed into Redwood Creek. The old trail led to a point right at the center of the fork. If I could make it to that spot, I'd be the first person to camp there in fifty-three years.

"Why'd they close the trail?" I asked.

The ranger shrugged. "It may have been too difficult to maintain. There could have been bear or mountain lion activity, flash floods or unstable redwoods."

I wondered if I could even find the trail. It'd certainly be a fascinating place for a solo backpacking trip. I love solo trips. John Muir said, "There's a silent voice in the wilderness that we hear only when no one else is around."

My first night was spent at Lodgepole Campground in Sequoia National Park. After setting up camp, I hoofed to the camp store for extra Coleman fluid and new rain gear. In the back of the freezer, I found a four-pack of Miller malt liquor in the red can with a golden eagle for $1.99. "Catch the Miller Malt Eagle," ads use to say. I hadn't seen one of these cans in ten years. I grabbed a couple.

At the counter, the teenage cashier rang it up. "A dollar ninety-nine," she said.

I looked up. "But it's a dollar ninety-nine for the four-pack."

"So?"

"So I'm only buying two."

She checked a list next to the register. "It says Miller malt singles are ninety-four cents plus tax."

"That makes no sense."

"Why not?"

I became exasperated. "So I can go back and get the other two from the four-pack for free?"

She thought long and hard about that one. "I guess."

It was a twelve-mile drive down a bumpy dirt road to Redwood Creek. At the trailhead, I rechecked my pack. Two girls with short hair and muscles hiked out of the woods and flopped their packs next to mine.

I said, "How was it back there?"

The bigger one said, "Cosmic. It was totally cosmic."

"Get much rain?"

"Lord, son," she said, indignantly. "You gotta expect rain in the Sierras."

The other one stared at me. "You think you're tough?"

I tilted my head. "Tough enough."

She smiled. "Don't let the bears bite."

The four-mile hike on Redwood Creek Loop was not difficult and traversed some of the most striking country on the planet. Nothing compares to the splendor of a mature redwood forest. I made it to the bridge in two hours. The creek was wide and swift, and the redwood groves were at their thickest. For the next hour, I was meticulous. I took ten to fifteen-foot swaths from the creek and bushwhacked fifty yards into the woods. It was slow and tiresome, and I could find no trace of the lost trail. Just when I was about to give up, I spotted a faded orange tin square nailed to a tree. I pushed through the brush for a closer inspection. It was definitely an old trail marker. I stared into the forest and squinted. In a moment or two, I saw another orange tin about thirty yards away. In between the markers were thickets, fallen logs and young redwoods. The trail was indeed gone, but the tin markers had survived.

I plunged into the wilderness and found the third marker. It was painfully slow going. Several times I was forced to crash forward and hope for the best. What should have been a leisurely forty-five minute stroll turned into a two-and-a-half-hour ordeal. It was nearly dark before I saw it. At the bottom of a hill was a flat clearing that straddled Redwood Creek and was flanked by two tributaries. A lip on the creek formed a twin waterfall.

After my tent was up and fire ablaze, I popped my first red can of Miller malt with the golden eagle. Unfortunately, malt liquor tastes like it's mixed with gasoline. My stomach percolated. I climbed into my tent and the twin waterfall was almost annoyingly loud.

Next morning I had my coffee by the river and began to re-read my dog-eared copy of *Desert Solitaire* by Edward Abbey. Suddenly, I didn't feel so hot. I stood up and took two steps – and there went my lunch. I'll spare the details, but needless to say I was miserable. I decided to hike back to my truck. The trip was going to be a death march.

Early on, I was forced to stop frequently. By this time it was coming out both ends. Food poisoning had to be the culprit, I decided. I did eat buffalo bacon at a café in Three Rivers the day before, but the Miller malt certainly didn't help. My vomiting eased up and I settled into a painstakingly slow but steady pace. After forty-five minutes, I looked up but couldn't locate an orange tin marker. I scanned every direction – nothing. Damn it – I'm an idiot! I must have wandered off the trail. Now I was hopelessly lost in a National Park wilderness. I took off my pack and sat down.

God – please just let me die right here and now.

After about twenty minutes of sulking, I rallied. Chin up, I told myself. Surrender was not an option. I turned on my heels and backtracked. In less than fifteen minutes, I spotted an orange tin square. Yes! I hugged the tree in relief.

Guess I was going to live for another day.

GK

Eight

Eccentricity

"I'd rather be a little weird than all boring."
- Rebecca McKinsey

"Originals cost more than imitations."
- Suzy Kassem

"I'm not an eccentric. It's just that I am more alive than most people. I am an unpopular electric eel set in a pond of catfish."
- Edith Sitwell

I WENT TO A PLAY a month ago. It was *Hamlet.* I went with three of my teacher buddies, all guys. My golf buddies, all guys, lost their minds when they found out I was giving up a night of great football games to go to the theater. Does that make me an eccentric? Unconventional? Slightly strange? Does it make them Neanderthal mouth-breathers? Not really sure on any of those questions but it leads to a discussion of what does make us feel alive. And as unconventional or even more-than-slightly strange it might be to admit, one of the things that makes me feel alive is Shakespeare. If those golf buddies saw this admission, their hair might catch on fire, but they're not literate, they'll never read this, so I'm safe and I can get on with it.

I have seen various interpretations of *Hamlet* in which the same actor played Hamlet and Hamlet's father's ghost, at the same time. Hellish and dark, smoke surrounding him/them, lamenting that "the serpent that did sting thy father now wears his crown." (Act 1 Sc. 5) The entire play was suffused with the music of Pink Floyd.

"The lunatic is in my head.

You raise the blade.

You make the change,

You rearrange me till I'm sane." (Pink Floyd: "Brain Damage")

Lunatic indeed. Sad, tragic Hamlet.

I have seen a particular opening of *Macbeth* where the theater is pitch dark and the only sound we hear is a metallic drip, drip, drip. The lights fade on and we see that the drips were actually blood falling from above onto what we can now see is a trap door. Moments later, the trap door opens and three gauze-covered ghostly witches come writhing out of the depths. It is these three "Weird Sisters" who will determine Macbeth's pathetic fate.

In the same play, Lady Macbeth is trying to wipe the kingly blood from her hands. She wipes the blood on the floor and when she stands and regards what she has done, what we all see is a perfect scarlet pentagram. "Out, out damned spot," she pleads. Damned indeed. Sad, tragic Macbeth and his unhinged wife.

So what is it about these plays, about Shakespeare, that still holds us? Liking Shakespeare, let alone loving Shakespeare wasn't easy. Remember our English teachers falling all over themselves, speaking breathlessly about the Bard's greatness? We had to listen about "groundlings," and probably even had to create some lame papier-mâché Globe Theater. Geez. But somewhere along the line, we finally were able to grasp the humanity involved in these stories. Yes, his characters are high-stationed VIP's: emperors, princes, kings, queens. But they are fragile and flawed, and being fragile and flawed ourselves we are still to this day drawn to them.

We see Brutus stare into the flame and hear his long-dead friend Caesar say to him: "to tell thee that thou shalt see me at Philippi." Brutus is reminded of his betrayal of his friend and knows he will soon pay the price for that betrayal. Betrayal is not only of the ancient times...and we are drawn in again. We see the aforementioned Hamlet, in probably Shakespeare's most famous soliloquy, ask life's hardest question:

> To be or not to be,
> That is the question.
> Whether 'tis nobler in the mind to suffer the slings
> and arrows of outrageous fortune,
> Or to take arms 'gainst a sea of troubles,
> And by opposing,
> End them.

To be or NOT to be. Two choices. To accept passively the unfairness of what life has just handed him, or to attempt to create a new normal? Our choices, our decisions on a daily basis? Surely not as dramatic or threatening as the Prince's choices. Our lives are not the stuff of which tragedy is made, and yet...

We are taught in school the difference between fiction and non-fiction. Some of these made-up characters do in fact have some historical standing. For the most part though, Shakespeare presented us with his own creations. So I return to the premise of this essay: do I feel more alive than most people because of Hamlet and Caesar and Macbeth and his conniving but crazy wife? Do I experience these men and their wives differently because I have spent my life in an English classroom? That might be so. And if that, in the words of Edith Sitwell, makes me an eccentric, I plead guilty. Because I simply could not have it any other way.

TC

MY WIFE'S AUNT JEAN was a genuine Florida eccentric.

After Elaine and I got married, we moved to Aunt Jean's home in Ocala, Florida so I could finish my degree at the University of Florida in Gainesville. Aunt Jean insisted we move into her small guesthouse for free. Aunt Jean and her late husband Jack had bought ten acres and established two businesses – The Rustic Hobby Nursery and Rustic Grill Restaurant. Aunt Jean gave us jobs at the restaurant. We each earned a free dinner and ten dollars a night. Elaine worked very hard. She bused the tables while my only duties were to pour (and drink) beer from behind the bar and man the register. I came home from my first day at school and parked at the nursery hoping to find Aunt Jean. I knew she liked to relax under a shady oak among all her plants. I found her on a bench, smoking Camels and drinking an Old Milwaukee beer.

"Can I interest you in some gardenias?" she asked.

"Jean," I said, "it's me Gary - Elaine's husband."

"Right," she said. "You're my little buddy." I was 6' and 175 pounds and she was barely 5' and 90 pounds, yet I was her little buddy.

"I want to thank you again for everything," I said. "The guesthouse is perfect and we both enjoy working at the restaurant."

"Wanna beer?"

"Not yet, thank you."

She eyeballed my car. It was a dark green 1970 340 Duster – and my pride and joy. "That clunker is too loud. I think you need a new muffler."

I tilted my head. "It's supposed to be loud. It's a V8 muscle car."

"Sounds to me like it needs a tune-up and new muffler. I know a good mechanic."

"I'll take you for a ride," I said. "You'll love it."

She took a gulp of beer. "You sure you kids are hitched?"

I smiled. "Yeah, we're married."

"You ain't bullshittin' me, are ya?"

"I'll show you the license."

"It's not God's way to shack up. You'll both go to hell if you're not hitched."

"I swear were married, Aunt Jean."

She finished her Camel and Old Milwaukee. "Then let's take a cruise in that hot rod."

I loved the Delmonico steaks at the Rustic Grill, but everything else was good too – chops, spaghetti, crab and fried shrimp. The restaurant opened at 3:00 p.m., but until 5:00 there were only beer drinkers. Elaine and I ate our dinners at 4:30 and then worked 5:00-10:00. Aunt Jean sat with us while we ate and played with her mechanical monkey. The beer drinkers loved that silly thing. At 5:00 she'd head for the kitchen and start to cook. She only had one set-up girl to help her. From 5:30-8:00 the place was bedlam, but from 8:00-10:00 the beer drinkers returned. When the place got real crazy, Aunt Jean would stick her head out of the kitchen and ask for an Old Milwaukee. It was the only beer on tap.

I brought her the beer. "Wow, I was looking at the pictures over the bar. Dan Blocker and Lorne Green ate here?"

"They were real cowboys," Aunt Jean said.

"And Lloyd Bridges?"

"They filmed *Seahunt* at Silver Springs. He usually brought his two sons. Oh, what obnoxious little bastards."

"They're both famous movie stars now."

My favorite picture was of Aunt Jean and her late husband Jack with heavyweight boxing champion Jack Dempsey. I loved the Manassas Mauler.

"No one ever picked a fight with him," Aunt Jean said.

"I wish I'd met him."

"Hell, Elvis Presley ate here twice."

I eyed her suspiciously. "You ain't bullshittin' me, are ya?"

"In 1962 he was filming *Follow That Dream* in downtown Ocala. Your little sweetie-pie had a big crush on him."

And so it went for eight months.

After my last day at school, I stopped at the restaurant for a beer. It was 3:30 p.m. and only a handful of beer drinkers sat in the booths.

"Hello there," Aunt Jean said.

"I'll take an Old Milwaukee."

The phone rang. Aunt Jean answered and said, "Just a minute." She looked all over the restaurant. "No," she said. "He ain't here." She listened for a moment and said, "Just a minute." She looked all over the restaurant again. "Just because his car's parked out front don' mean he's here." She hung up.

"I finished my degree today," I said. "I couldn't have done it without your help."

Aunt Jean stared at me.

"Oh, shit," she said. "I just told Elaine you weren't here."

Yep. My wife's Aunt Jean was a genuine Florida eccentric.

GK

Nine

Quests

*"Say the word 'quest' out loud. It is an
extraordinary word, isn't it? So small and
yet so full of wonder, so full of hope."*
 - Kate Dicamillo

*"You didn't get the quest you wanted,
you got the one you could do."*
 - Lev Grossman

AT TIMES I AM to camping what Clark Griswold is to the concept of vacation. I have to admit that there have been some Keystone Kop-esque miscues and misadventures on some of the quests I've undertaken with my buddies. So even the idea, borrowing Lev Grossman's thought, that I got the one (quest) I could do, is pushing it. I've "gotten" and taken hikes and been on camping trips that I clearly COULDN'T do, that clearly demanded more skill than I possessed, but there was always some form of magic, of discovery, of exploration, in each one.

And so my idea for this section will be to paint a few thumbnail images of my forays, my quests, into the great beyond…OK, it really wasn't "beyond" all that much. A few states away will have to suffice; you get the picture.

1. Dad of The Year: (Pat's Island)

I never camped as a kid, wasn't a Boy Scout, and even as an adult could barely put up a simple tent without help. With that vaunted outdoor experience, I decided to take my four and six-year-old sons camping to a beautiful camping area just out of town called Pat's Island in the Ocala National Forest. No water near this island, just a raised stand of pine trees and majestic oaks. I knew the boys would love it...and they did...until 10:00 p.m. We were watching the fire disappear to embers, getting ready to call it a night and hit the sleeping bags. Then we heard the bear.

Actually I heard the bear and hoped beyond hope that my sons Jared and Dustin had not. They had. A few hundred yards away from our tents, something large was making its presence known. Little boys do not hide fear well. I tried for two minutes to explain away the sound. Passing jets overhead is one of the lamer things I came up with. Good try, Dad of the year.

We broke camp, put our stuff in the little red wagon we all thought was so cute just hours earlier, and we hiked out by 11:00 p.m. By 12:30 they were asleep in their own beds. My sons are now thirty and thirty-two years old and they love camping. Of course they do.

2. Husband of the Year: (My white cup)

I drink gin.

Eight years ago when I got married, our pastor who performed the ceremony gave Mary and me a flower arrangement. It was a collection of...who am I kidding – I have no idea what the flowers were, but it was the kind of arrangement that had a tall thin cup that held all the flowers. A tall, white plastic cup. When we took all the flowers home from the church the next day, for the first time I noticed that cup. It turned out to be the perfect sixteen-ounce gin and tonic cup.

What does this have to do with camping? This white plastic holder of flowers became my go-to cup on all of our camping trips. It became a gag with my buddies; we couldn't leave for the trip until they saw that cup. I used it religiously (see what I did there?) on every hiking and camping trip a solid seven years, until it finally cracked and disintegrated from overuse. I'm sure it was the wear and tear of being packed and unpacked that caused its demise. I mean, how much gin would it take to break down plastic? That is what I call a solid wedding present.

3. Hidden Pond (part one): Who nearly dies from cold in Florida?

The guys I camp with are legit campers. I'm a pretender. Nearly every bit of my camping equipment, ok, literally every bit of my camping equipment, except my white cup, is of hand-me-down variety. So I do pretty well "out there" thanks to their generosity. Except for the clothing, and the sleeping bag. These are all mine. Winter camping for me simply entails jamming a few more sweaters and sweatshirts into my already badly planned backpack. Bulky sweat pants are worn under my jeans. I do buy a few of those magic packets that warm up when you smack them. My gloves are tan suede with thinning lining. I know – a recipe for disaster.

Gary and I went for a one-night stay to one of the most beautiful spots in the entire Ocala National Forest: Hidden Pond. The temperature on the three-and-a-half-mile hike out through pine and oak was an exhilarating fifty to fifty-five degrees with a pure Florida winter blue sky. It was that night that I almost became an embarrassing statistic death by freezing in Florida. By midnight, the temperature had dropped well below freezing, into the teens. You know that chill when your core is cold, when your teeth chatter and your hands shake. That cold. Those magic heat packets did nothing. My extra-thick Gator sweatshirt? Nope. My "Good down to forty degrees Fahrenheit" sleeping bag? Death...a sad, shameful, "who dies from the cold in Florida" type of death became a possibility.

Meanwhile, as he later told me, Gary had shed his vest and pants, because he was TOO HOT in his sleeping bag. Thirty feet away from my tent, cold as a meat locker, my buddy was near-naked and sweating. Nice one.

When even the fetal position brought me no respite from the cold, I stumbled out of the tent, determined to at least die trying to survive. I could hear Dylan Thomas... "rage, rage against the dying of the light." No – that's a lie, I was just freezing my ass off. I managed to re-start our fire, difficult as that was because my hands were borderline useless nubs. And so, next to this life-renewing fire, I fell asleep in my lawn chair. (Yes I bring lawn chairs on camping trips – don't judge.)

When Gary came out of his tent just after sunrise, he said, "How'd you sleep, Honk?" Yes – he calls me "Honk." Don't ask.

I told him to go screw himself and nodded off.

4. Hidden Pond (part two): "So this
naked guy walks into our camp…"

His name was Harold. He had on a beret, topsiders, and a gold chain around his neck. And. Nothing. Else.

The day before this event, a couple of us had been walking around, wandering if you will, a ways from our tents and we met some guys who turned out to be Harold's friends. One of us had brought along a bottle of wine; the other had brought a bottle of beer. We talked for a few minutes, found out that the third member of their party was indeed named Harold, and then we said goodbye. But this really isn't about the day before.

The next morning, Harold, as I just mentioned, walks into our camp talking about wanting to meet "Chardonnay Guy and Beer Man." Now, it is coffee-time early, and we are hung over and sitting in our chairs shaking off the night's sleep. I'm slumped in my own chair, waiting for somebody to bring me that coffee, and he appears right next to me. Let's review. I'm slumped in my chair. Harold is standing next to me. Want to guess what was basically right at eye level? Yep. THAT.

That's it. That's the whole story. A naked guy walks into a camp full of guys he doesn't know, in the middle of a forest miles from anything. If Harold had chosen the wrong group of campers, he'd have been buried and forgotten. But he chose us and now his legend grows with each new re-telling of the naked dude who walked into our camp and lived to tell about it.

5. My first camping trip: Brother –
   can you spare a bungee cord?

I like cold drinks. I think that is one of the reasons I had never camped until I was well into my thirties. So when most real men made their maiden (real men...maiden?) camping trips as youngsters, I had, as an adult not strayed far from the ice machine.

All this merely to say, to no one's surprise, that my first real, out-of-state trip did not go swimmingly. At 6,600 feet, Clingmans Dome is the highest point in the Tennessee Smoky Mountains. I have written about my camping prowess, or lack thereof, but this time the problem was that there was a fairly intense hike before I got to the camping stage. So this happened. The first quarter of a mile from the trailhead was practically straight downhill. I hadn't made it fifty feet when my boot slipped, I staggered and every bit of the shit in my pack fell out and tumbled away into the bushes and down the trail. "Man down" is a line that should be reserved for men who take huge risks: policemen, firemen, military men. But here I am, a thirty-something English teacher who can't make it two minutes before he has to call for three of his friends to help him get back to vertical. And locate his scattered stuff. Camper Extraordinaire? Not so much.

Almost thirty years later, I'd like to report that I am not a whit better at the whole hiking/camping thing. But I do have a well-known nickname that I embrace. I am "Bungee Man." Who needs to pack efficiently when seven bungee cords secure all that I might need for the next three nights?

6.   Bear in the camp: "There's been an incident."

In the northern Great Smoky Mountains of Tennessee is an area called Porter's Creek. Though the hike itself is worth discussing, it is the brief time we spent there that is the topic at hand.

The first night we camped, my friend Rob, (nicknamed Robo! by Gary and yes he says Robo loudly – thus the exclamation mark) heated up some freeze-dried beef stew he had packed in. It wasn't only the taste that made it incredible, miles away from civilization, but it was the smell. And it was the smell of that beef stew that started a chain reaction which changed our plans.

It was the next afternoon that the bear came. We spotted him, well-distant at first, but within an hour or so, he was in our camp. What I mean by "in our camp," is that he got inside of what I call The Circle of Caring, inside the tent area. Clearly we had a dilemma. We could stay but we were pretty sure he had friends. Sleep was probably out of the question. He had already gnarled my water bottle, which actually held flavored vodka (Firefox Lemmon Vodka – I give it my highest recommendation). He had not been fazed by our suggestions that he leave.

So late in the day, as it was getting dark, we decided to break camp and retrace our steps, a full day before we were supposed to leave. On the way, we noticed a bear trap we had not seen before. Who looks to the side when you're sucking wind on the way up a mountain? It was a difficult trek back down because we looked back constantly over our shoulders making sure our friend wasn't following, looking for more beef stew. We made it to the truck and drove to Gatlinburg where we found a cheap motel, the

Sleepy Bear Hotel. (No really – look it up.) When we had cell service again, Gary called home, got the answering machine, and left his wife this exact message: "We had to hike out early. There's been an incident." Click. End of message.

I'm not trying to call this ordeal a near-death experience but who would leave THAT message?

I need to re-evaluate who I hang out with.

7.   Black and white photos
     from a sometime camper.

Black and white photography has always intrigued me. It simplifies, it purifies, it leaves only the unadorned image. I have a number of brief memories, snippets, if you will, that come to me as black and white moments. They don't mean any less than the others I have detailed more intricately. They just seem a different part of my camping experience.

I've never camped at any great altitude; I've never awakened with snow on my sleeping bag. I've also never rappelled down a sheer rock face. But what I have done is stored frozen moments from so many of my less than dramatic trips; they all seem part of one long one. One long black and white Polaroid.

Years ago I walked back to our car, just a couple of miles away from our tents, just after we had put our tents up. Odd timing right? Why'd I go back? To get lawn chairs. I decided, dammit, that I was going to be comfortable out there in the semi-wild, and not sit on logs or dirt or roots. And now all my wizened camping friends somehow strap (bungee) their own chairs to their packs on our trips. You're welcome.

Drinking and camping. I plead guilty. Near Cherokee, North Carolina one night I had been drinking gin and thought it would be a good idea to go for a walk near the side of a bluff. I tripped and started sliding toward what I sensed would not be A SOFT LANDING. I was able to grab the base of a bush as I tumbled near the very edge. Spinal fusion averted. I still drink gin on camping trips, but my buds tell me to sit the hell down if it looks like I might do something stupid. Thanks, boys.

In the Smokies once, we slid down the slick side of a rock face that looked much like a flume at a water park. But at water parks, the water you plunge into is crystal clear. What we didn't see as we plummeted down the side of this rock were jagged iron railroad ties long submerged just under the surface. Puncture wounds from rusted iron and a three-hour hike to anything resembling a care center is what likely lay ahead for us. The two thoughts that simultaneously struck me as I struck the hidden danger were: what are those doing out here in the middle of the wilderness? And: I wonder if I should have checked the water first? There was no gin involved in this event.

At some point in my outdoor history, I camped on the same weekend with a guy who wore topsiders and carried the rest of his stuff in a duffel bag, and with two guys who BOTH forgot their tents. They had to sleep in someone else's. We now call the first guy the Indoorsman. I can't tell you what we call the other two.

One of my final favorite black and whites is as simple as it is corny. My wife and I are empty-nesters and we usually have company for the holidays. One Thanksgiving a few years ago, we realized none of our four kids were coming home. Our response was to pack a cooler with turkey and dressing and beer and head to the Ocala National Forest. The cooler was our table, we had lawn chairs (of course) and paper plates and plastic ware. What is the name of that chemical in turkey that makes you sleepy? The turkey and the beer and the wind soughing through the pines...that particular afternoon nap was one for the ages, and one for the aged.

I constantly play back these memories, opening the photo album to these moments and a hundred others like them. My times in the forest and on the trails and in the mountains. They could be, as I said, all part of one long trip. I know they aren't but they could be, and all of it collectively is a thread that runs through me and occasionally leads me back for more.

8. Moonrise over Zay Prairie:
Some concluding remarks
on quests that I could do.

I've been to Hawaii a half-dozen times, a fatherly benefit of having a son half a world away. And it never fails. I get up that first morning, completely jet-lagged, and head down to Waimanalo Bay or Kailua Bay to take a picture of the sunrise. Every time. Each sunrise is stunning in every way you would think a Hawaiian sunrise would be...that is until I get the picture back. Maybe it's the frame. Maybe it's what is NOT seen outside the lens view. Maybe it's the sound no still picture can ever duplicate. I don't know. But I do know what I'll be doing the first morning of my next quest in the Pacific paradise.

Back to camping. The camping itself is one thing; the storytelling after is something else. And so I'll end this by trying to describe a moonrise that was, not surprisingly, beyond description.

Zay Prairie is not far out of town but this night it felt other worldly. We knew there was to be a giant moon this night, but none of us had ever experienced anything like this. We saw it first, well below the treetops, a pale ghost of what it would become. I understand that all of us in our own way succumb to hyperbole, the sad result, maybe, of trying to describe the impossible. And yet, I had never been mesmerized by nature quite like this. We waited and watched. Waited and watched for it to climb those distant trees and break free. It took, hell, I have no idea how long it took. There are moments when time and place are meaningless – things just ARE.

Then there it was. Overlarge with its reflection gazing back up at it from the forest pond right in front of us. Grown men, used to guffawing and being childish goofballs, were silent, in near-supplication to what we now beheld. Then it was over. No, the moon was still there of course. But that moment, that very second it made its way into the ocean of the night sky, now too distant from us. That's what was over.

But it's never over. Not for a camper. Not for an observer. Sure, there is a bitter sweetness about it at times. It is the frame that does that. But the Hawaiian sunrises, the moonrises anywhere. The bears. The rock slides. The lawn chairs. Harold...even Harold. Lev Grossman seemed to infer that we can't get the quests that we can both want

AND do. I beg to differ, Lev, and I have a lifetime of trips to prove it.

TC

MY BROTHER CHRIS and I hiked out of the Santa Barbara River complex in the Pecos Wilderness section of the Santa Fe National Forest in New Mexico. In the beginning, I feared we wouldn't even be able to spend a night. The forest had an early November chill and a smattering of snow. When we were two miles up the trail, it began to rain.

I looked at the sky and asked, "What do you think?"

Chris wiped his eyes with his shirt. "It's freezing," he said. "Let's get outta here. This sucks."

At that moment, three backpackers appeared, hiking their way out. It was a father and two pre-teenage daughters.

"How was it back there?" I asked.

Dad grinned. "Magnificent. It was our best backpack ever."

"We had the river all to ourselves," the taller girl chirped.

"I wish we could've stayed another night," said the other.

They marched down the trail and I looked at Chris. "Let's get outta here," I mimicked.

He shrugged.

"Wuss," I said.

He wiped his eyes again. "Did you call me a wuss?

After three glorious nights, we hiked out. Our plan was to head for Santa Fe, clean up, and then venture out on a "quest for the holy margarita." The picturesque hamlet of Dixon was up ahead with the sparkling Embudo River running through it.

"Dixon's a tiny town with more chickens and burros than people," I said. "I'll show you where the Embudo flows into the Rio Grande."

We turned a corner and saw hundreds of cars parked along the highway and a throng of people jamming the streets. Turned out it was the annual Dixon Studio Tour with artists galore.

I bought a hand-carved wooden angel for fifty bucks.

Chris shook his head. "I can't believe you paid that much for a little piece of wood."

"They guy has a studio in Cordova," I said. "The woodcarvers of Cordova are legendary."

"Sucker."

La Chiripada Winery charged six dollars for a wine glass and unlimited tasting.

"This looks like fun."

"Don't you drink a drop," Chris said. "We're saving it for the holy margarita quest."

I wanted to stop at the El Santuario de Chimayo church, a famous contemporary pilgrimage site that has been called "no doubt the most important Catholic pilgrimage center in the United States." A small room off the main church contained a round pit which was the source of "holy dirt" that is believed to have healing powers. An adjacent room displayed discarded crutches and other testimonials from the reportedly healed. I stuffed a pinch of holy dirt into my shirt pocket for luck on our holy quest.

In Santa Fe, we parked at the Hotel St. Francis on Don Gaspar Street, a few blocks from the historic and iconic plaza. It was only 3:00 p.m. and our room wasn't quite ready.

"You can wait in the bar," the reservationist suggested.

Chris smiled. "Our quest for the holy margarita begins."

We dropped our packs in the tiny bar and ordered the silver *especiale.*

I took a sip. "OMG! This is good. Superb margarita."

"Don't be such a doofus," Chris said. "We're going to be sampling the best of the best on the plaza. This margarita is okay, but I doubt she'll measure up with the big boys."

"Did you call me a doofus?"

We walked upstairs to the Ore House with its incredible view of the plaza. The waiter brought complimentary nachos and dipping cheese with our margaritas.

I took a sip. "Too much ice."

"Way too watery," Chris said.

"Aren't you going to finish it?"

"Nope. We gotta pace ourselves."

We stopped at the north end of the plaza to buy presents for our wives from the Native American artists. Their wares were spread out on blankets. I found a delicate silver bracelet with turquoise stones.

I smiled at the lady. "How much?"

She didn't look at me. "Fifty dollars.

Must be the standard price, I decided. "What do you have for twenty-five?"

She pointed to another row.

"Thanks anyway." I started to walk away.

"Forty dollars," she said.

I stopped. "I can only spare thirty-five. My brother and I are on a quest for the holy margarita."

For the first time she smiled. "Deal."

The lobby at the La Fonda Hotel was impressive. It had a magnificent restaurant with a glass ceiling. We took the elevator to the Bell Tower Bar on the roof and enjoyed a panoramic view of downtown. The traditional margarita with no ice was delicious. I asked our server where the locals go for margaritas.

She said, "Pandora's on Old Pecos Trail. They serve margarita jugs – three or four drinks."

At Pandora's, I took one sip and nearly puked. "It tastes like sangria with tequila."

"Time to go to Shangri-La," Chris said, referring to the El Dorado Hotel. The El Dorado was the only five-star hotel in the state of New Mexico.

We sat at the bar and sampled the *El Perfecto*. "Very good," I said, "but…"

Chris nodded and said, "I know – it has no personality."

"What do you wanna do?"

"I want to have a holy margarita," he said, "and I've made my choice."

I said, "Me too."

We headed back to the tiny bar at the Hotel St. Francis.

GK

Ten

Haunting

"If you're not haunted by something, as by a dream, a vision, or a memory...you're not interested or even involved."
- Jack Kerouac

REFLECTIONS ON *NOT* being a teacher.

Which of these statements is not like the others?

...end of class

...end of the unit

...end of the quarter

...end of the semester

...end of the faculty meeting

...end of my career

I have been reflecting lately about what it might be like to not be a teacher. Actually, the word "might" is not accurate. Fact is, I will NOT be a teacher in three years. I signed papers a couple of summers ago that did two things: it gained me extra money for retirement, and it gave me five more years to work. After that fifth year I have to retire or will lose that money. And so, there is an hourglass somewhere with five years' worth of sand that is slowly by inexorably running out. Am I haunted by this vision, by this foreknowledge of what will be? No. Not yet anyway. This essay I assume is going to be an exploration of what that might feel like. My friend Ray Bradbury used to say that he would start a story and just sit back and see where his characters lead him. I sense these reflections will follow a similar path.

This is new ground for me. I have taught English for thirty-four years; it will be a total of thirty-seven when I call it a career in June 2020. I have never voluntarily left something that I have loved – like I said – new ground. And I am going to try to not sound morose but it will be hard to put an objective slant on something I have done passionately for well over half of my life. I don't know if mailmen, or architects, or widget salesmen are reflective as their careers wind down, but that is certainly where I find myself.

And so in no particular order, these are some of the things I will miss about teaching...

- Friday afternoon of three-day weekends
- Spring Break
- The energy of twenty-five seventeen-year-olds discussing how $2 + 2 = 5$
- My classroom which thirty-four years has turned into a museum
- Handing out my Parrot Head Awards
- College acceptance day for my seniors
- The International Baccalaureate Program
- Discussing nerdy teacher nuances with nerdy English teachers
- Kids. I will miss kids.
- Scout and Atticus. Nora. Winston Smith. Amir and Hassan. John Isidore. Hazell Motes. Ethan Hawley.

Harrison Bergeron. Guy Montag. Prince Hamlet and poor pathetic Ophelia. Jolly Mon. Sarah Sylvia Cynthia Stout (who just could not take the garbage out). Scout…I know I mentioned her already, but if you've ever taught *To Kill A Mockingbird,* you'd miss her enough to mention her twice… And every other character inside the cover of a book that has allowed me to enter their lives for all these years.

- Reading my rejection letters to my students
- My former students coming back to visit me in their old classroom
- Talking to kids before school who come by because they need a sounding board
- Being nervous on the first day of school
- Being sad on the last day of school

And so on…

I talk with my students a lot about passion, about whether or not they will feel drawn to a particular vocation as if it's a calling. Of course I want them to find an 8 AM to 5 PM existence that is as meaningful as my 7:30 AM to 3 PM existence has been to me. But being seniors in high school, they sense that making a living might be less than a passion or a calling, and for that I am sorry for them.

But that's ok, because this isn't about them, it's about me. It's odd that what is supposed to be merely a job takes on a separate type of meaning. It becomes organic; it takes on a life of its own. It becomes a living thing. And I guess it's that idea of a living thing that has me a bit concerned, even three years out. When that previously mentioned hourglass drops its final grain of sand, the life that I have lead for all these years will simply not exist. The first day of school in August 2020 will be the first time since the fall of 1983 that I will not have a classroom to go to. Speaking of that day, the one plan I actually do have for retirement is that I am going to be out of town for the first three weeks of that school year. I don't handle sadness and loss well, and that particular point in time might include both of these emotions. I simply will need to be gone.

As my friend Kurt Vonnegut said over and over again in *Slaughterhouse Five* – "so it goes."

I knew I loved English. I knew I loved kids. I did not know I would love teaching. But at the mid-point of more summers than not, I would feel an antsy-ness, a dis-ease, an emptiness even, and I realized it was because I hadn't been a teacher for a month and a half. I felt unemployed. Then five weeks later summer would be over, and I would be back in my element. In three years, I will need a new element. To say that I am bothered to the point of being haunted by this would be overstating it a bit, but as I like to say – it certainly has my attention.

I'll end with this. In my list of things I'll miss when my teaching days are done, I mentioned former students coming back to visit. When the classroom door opens and one (or four or five as is often the case) walks in, I don't tell them, "Welcome back." Instead I say, "Welcome home." And that's what classrooms and kids and books and writing have been to me since I was twenty-eight years old. Home. That's a significant void to fill.

I've got three years to figure how to do that.

TC

MY WIFE ELAINE'S best friend Sandy Finley owned a strikingly beautiful two-story house in the historic district of St. Augustine, Florida. It was located on Cincinnati Street and within walking distance of downtown and the iconic Spanish fort.

St. Augustine is the oldest continuously occupied European-established city in the contiguous United States. It was founded in 1565 and was forty years ahead of Jamestown. The town is resplendent and obviously loaded with history. Haunted too.

At Christmas, Sandy visited her mother in Miami. She offered her house to us for the week. It was a great deal for everyone – we had a free place to stay, nicer than any hotel, and Sandy had pet sitters for her four cats and big collie. We jumped at the opportunity.

The house had twelve-foot ceilings, vintage crown molding and heart of pine wood floors. Upstairs were the master bedroom, den and a tiny six-by-eight-foot office. Sandy called it her "little room." It was too claustrophobic for Elaine and me. A breezy screened-in porch was off the master bedroom.

Our first night we ate at the Columbia Restaurant on St. George and Hypolita Streets and then splurged on a gourmet popsicle from a vendor in the park. Back at the house, I took Sophie the collie for a long walk. At bedtime, Sophie refused to come upstairs. Nothing could persuade her to join us. I even offered a rib from the Columbia. I brought a water bottle upstairs and placed it on a small wooden chair next to the bed.

All four cats slept with us.

I woke up and heard giggling. I got up to go to the bathroom and the giggling stopped. My water bottle was missing.

"What's the matter?" Elaine asked.

"Did you move my water bottle?"

"No," she said. "You leave those things all over the house."

"Did you hear giggling?"

"No."

I went to the bathroom. The door was to the "little room" was ajar. I pushed the door open and turned on the light. Nothing.

In the morning, Elaine said, "I found your water bottle. It was on the stair bannister."

Next evening we took Sophie to the Castillo de San Marcos fort and watched the rangers fire the cannons. It was a perfect night – clear, cool and refreshing. At the house, I let Sophie inside and Elaine and I sat on the front covered porch and drank wine. When I went to pour us another glass, the screen door was locked.

"What the hell is this?" I said.

"What?"

"The screen door is locked."

At that moment, a police car cruised by and I waved for them to stop. The policemen were very friendly.

"I let the dog inside and now the screen door is locked."

"Maybe the dog scratched at the door and hit the handle," the first officer said.

"But it has a little key," I said.

They got out of their car.

"Maybe one of you locked the screen and went out the back door."

"Nope," Elaine said and pointed. "Look down the hall."

We all looked. The back door had a vertical rod door jammer on it.

The policemen herded us back and drew their guns. After a thorough search of the house, they shrugged their shoulders.

"I still think it was the collie," the first one said.

We went to bed. I placed my water bottle on the small wooden chair next to the bed. All four cats slept with us. I awoke and heard voices. It sounded like a group of people talking in the street. I reached for my water bottle and discovered it was missing. Sure enough, it was back on the stair bannister. A soft glow downstairs told me the television was on.

"What is it?" Elaine said loudly. I leaped into the air.

"Jesus, you didn't have to sneak up on me," I said. "The TV is on."

"Maybe Sandy has it on a timer," Elaine said.

"I guess."

In the morning we had a great time taking Sophie on a tour of Flagler College. It had once been the luxurious Flagler Hotel. We ate blackened shrimp for dinner at the A1A Ale Works on King Street and headed home.

I took Sophie for a short walk. When I returned, Elaine was rattled.

"I heard giggling in the 'little room.'"

"It probably came from next door."

"I don't think so."

I woke up and my water bottle was missing again. A black shadow crossed the room and went through a wall. I leaped out of bed.

"What's wrong?" Elaine yelped.

"I saw something."

All four cats had disappeared.

Footsteps thumped in the hallway. I opened the door and turned on the light. Nothing. My water bottle sat on the stair bannister. The moment I got back in bed, footsteps thumped in the hallway again. A giggle came from the "little room."

"Maybe we should go to the Super 8," Elaine said.

In the morning, Elaine called Sandy to tell her we were moving to a motel.

"Are you okay?" Sandy asked. "You sound a little stressed."

Elaine said, "Well..."

"Did you see the little man sitting in the wood chair next to the bed?" she asked.

"Little man?"

"He's a sweet little ghost," Sandy claimed, "although he does like to play pranks."

GK

Eleven

Fear

*"Expose yourself to your deepest fears;
after that, fear has no power, and the fear
shrinks and vanishes."*

- Jim Morrison

GEORGE ORWELL'S 1984 – A guide to the first two decades of the 21st century.

It is relatively common knowledge that George Orwell did not intend his novel 1984 to be a prediction, i.e., a year by which what he writes about in his book, comes true. Rather, he meant it as a warning. I do believe his warning WAS meant to scare us, to put not necessarily the fear of God in us, but certainly the fear of Big Brother, in whatever form he might take. His words: "...it is a show-up of the perversions to which a centralized (government) is liable..." (p. 145, *A Reader's Guide to George Orwell*. Jeffrey Meyers. Littlefield, Adams and Co., Totowa, NJ, 1977). I say this not to try to sell books for him. I say this simply to remind us that even though the YEAR 1984 is far distant in the rear-view, the BOOK 1984 is still relevant. And it is on the book's relevance I'd like to start this essay.

JOHNNY GOT HIS GUN, TO KILL A MOCKINGBIRD, FAHRENHEIT 451, JONATHON

LIVINGSTON SEAGULL, WALDEN. If we consider ourselves readers, these (and of course many more) are books that must be read. They appeal to the romantic in us, the idealist in us. They appeal to the part in us that has not become too jaded or too world-weary as we turn calendar pages. To this list I add the aforementioned 1984.

We all love enemies and great literature provides us with enemies we love to hate. In Trumbo's JOHNNY GOT HIS GUN, the enemy is "you masters of men who plan the wars and point the way." In TO KILL A MOCKINGBIRD, the enemy is "Maycomb's usual disease," which is of course prejudice. In FAHRENHEIT 451, it is the "solid unmoving cattle of the majority." In WALDEN, the enemy is the "life of quiet desperation" that the masses of men lead. These books too, I would argue, are still extremely timely, though their publishing dates are decades ago. But back to 1984. What is a more mysterious and sinister enemy than Big Brother? And since every enemy creates underdogs, where in literature is there more of an underdog than Winston Smith, fighting his solitary fight against the omnipotent Big Brother, knowing his efforts had to end with his utter personal defeat? But underdogs also create empathy in us and empathy breeds hope. All readers need hope.

These two opposing concepts, the enemy that saps the strength of our protagonist and the hope that Winston can win the un-winnable...these concepts are what drive my observations here. There are moments of despair and moments of possibility in 1984. That sounds a great deal like what we have experienced on a regular basis early on in this century. My plan is to use Orwell's own words from

1984 as a vehicle to discuss some of what we're about today.

"Orthodoxy is unconsciousness."

"2 + 2 = 5."

In Orwell's Oceania the only religion was Big Brother. If he said that two and two made five, then that was the gospel of the day. Penalties for bucking that system were almost unimaginable. People were made into an "unperson" (a person who never existed) or subjected to their worst fear. For Winston it was rats on his face. I digress. The point is that the people were beaten into submission, and submit was all they could do.

Today, while the penalties are obviously less severe, the numbers of ideas that are deemed punishable are manifold. That is sad because, besides keeping within the confines of what is legal, shouldn't each of us be allowed to determine what our own orthodoxy is? I have a poster of the First Amendment in my classroom which outlines our incredible freedoms when it comes to expression. Speech. Religion. Assembly. There are freedoms at the micro level, the personal level. And they should be sacred. We won't shatter as a nation if someone defies accepted orthodoxy. The tenets of the First Amendment are strong enough to stand up to the individual rights promised to us, even if those rights aren't in line with the loudest voices. No government, or party or macro organization should demand unconsciousness as a price for being accepted; the longterm results would be devastating. Demand that two and two make four, even in the face of authority who might say otherwise.

"If there is hope, it lies in the proles."

In 1984, Orwell created an underclass, the proletariat, the proles, who were essentially the great unwashed. Winston needed hope that one day the structure of Big Brother's oligarchy could be defeated. The proles, massive in numbers, but for the most part ignored, were his hope.

I have taught in a public high school, actually two public high schools, for thirty-four years, and for me the hope lies in our kids. Unlike Orwell's proles, our young people are not the great unwashed, but they are at times forgotten or at least disregarded. I willingly and freely admit my bias of loving my students. Even though these same young people wander around with their noses stuck in their phones, I simple choose to see more than that and I wish my older brethren (and sistren?) could look past that, too. My kids ask incredible questions and where there is questioning there is curiosity. We want our young people to be curious. They invite me to their weddings, and they call me when they have a baby, although they sometimes get the order of those events wrong. They read my body language on my rare bad days, and they ask me what they can do to help. They are empathetic. We want our young people to be interested in more than what they see in the mirror each morning. They have made me, just one of dozens of teachers they've had, a part of their lives. They understand that they are part of a really cool continuum. We want them to trust in those who have come before them.

In 1984, there was no prole revolution. Winston's hope was never realized. Mine will be though, because I am wildly optimistic about where our young people will lead us.

"The invention of print made it easier to manipulate public opinion…with the development of television and the technical advancement which made it possible to receive and transmit simultaneously on the same instrument, private life came to an end."

The phrase "Big Brother is watching you" is ubiquitous. In the book though, it isn't really Big Brother watching; it is his Thought Police watching through the telescreen. The telescreen is the instrument that transmits and receives simultaneously and it is what ultimately is used to catch most thought criminals. That is why everyone in the fictional Oceania has to assume they are always being watched and listened to…thus – no private lives.

This similarity to what we do and have today is haunting. But the major difference is stark and it is an indictment against us all. In Oceania the invasion of privacy was done TO them by Big Brother. Here today, we have done it intentionally to ourselves. We can't go ten minutes without posting where we are and what we are doing. We can't walk to the mailbox without our phones lest we miss a call from the president asking our advice on the nuances of his trade policy. We have turned attention whores into reality stars, because…because we want to see someone as flawed and awkward as we are on national TV? We even have a new president who finds it necessary to Tweet out his grand proclamations at 5:00 a.m.…and we pay attention. Absurd.

Winston Smith was a victim. The Party was omnipotent and omnipresent and the telescreen was its eyes and ears. Yet the death wound of OUR private lives was self-inflicted. How did we ever think that publishing, uncensored, everything about ourselves was a good idea? I don't know if collective narcissism is a thing but when we look for someone to blame, our next selfie will reveal the offender.

"He bent down and began picking some, partly to pass the time away but also from the vague idea that he would like to have a bunch of flowers to offer the girl when they met."

1984 is a book with few moments of hope, but this is one of them. Winston meets a girl, her name is Julia but he doesn't even know her name yet. This is the first moment they are to be together, away from the telescreen's prying eyes... so he gets her flowers. In a world where there is neither dignity nor pride nor selflessness, he thinks he should greet her with flowers when she arrives. How does that happen? What makes Winston sense what he should do?

Here is the answer. There was something in him and there is something in us that KNOWS. Late in the book, Winston, in a moment sadly more dire for him than this flower moment, calls this goodness "the spirit of man." There is something ancestral, innate, inherent, something from what I would call the "before-times," that makes us understand when decency and kindness are called for. Have you ever seen a young boy hold a door open for an old woman who is not his granny? Have you seen a teacher stay after school until dark tutoring kids, who are not her students, so they have a chance to pass a state test? Have you seen an older brother let his younger brother cross the finish line first? What "finish line"? Any finish line, and that little brother will remember that "victory" for the rest of his life.

So what have we observed here? This was not meant to be a book review. God knows I could do that, having taught this book since, let's review, 1984. The title of this essay suggested this was to be a guide to the beginning of the 21st century and I see now that might not be completely accurate. But what IS accurate is what that book reveals to us about us. It shows the pettiness and the shallowness of what we too often have allowed ourselves to become; it shows what fear can do to us. It also, albeit briefly, shows the wonder of which we are capable. In the fictional Oceania, Winston loses his battle when he realizes that two and two DOES make five, just like Big Brother said it always had. But like Walter Cronkite said of the success of this book…it failed as a prediction because it succeeded as a warning. This book at times offers us a nightmare scenario of what the future, our future, could be. But it doesn't have to be that way. Fictional boogiemen don't define us. Our hope does. So bring on the next part of this new century.

TC

WHICH IS THE SCARIEST movie of all-time? Obviously, a film that exposes our deepest fears and dread must be in the running. Any discussion of scary movies must begin with the Universal Studios early classics such as *Dracula* (1931) with Bela Lugosi, *Frankenstein* (1931) with Boris Karloff and *The Wolf Man* (1941) with Lon Chaney. All are worthy of consideration, but none are truly nightmarish. The creepiest and most disturbing Karloff and Lugosi vehicle is *The Body Snatcher* (1945), based on a short story by Robert Louis Stevenson. Karloff was finally given the opportunity to act, rather than just wave his arms and snarl. His performance was a memorable portrayal of pure evil with a cheerful grin.

Next we should consider *Psycho* (1960) with Anthony Perkins, *Rosemary's Baby* (1969) with Mia Farrow, *The Exorcist* (1973) with Ellen Burstyn and Linda Blair, and *The Omen* (1976) with Gregory Peck and Lee Remick. All are horrifying and must be rated in the top ten, but – come on – the devil doesn't really exist and most guys I know believe they could easily bitch-slap Perkins. Let's not forget John Carpenter's *Halloween* (1979). It initiated the cult slasher genre and Jamie Lee Curtis is undeniably hot. It's also very scary.

Finally, there's *The Shining* (1980) with Jack Nicholson, *Silence of the Lambs* (1991) with Anthony Hopkins and Jodie Foster, and newer additions like *The Ring* (2002) with Naomi Watts and *The Conjuring* (2013) with Vera Farmiga.

But hold on.

Before you pick your favorite, please allow me to offer up my choice for the scariest and most terrifying movie of all-time – John Boorman's *Deliverance* (1972). The film is a harrowing experience that plays on man's darkest fears. It is also a daytime nightmare that takes place in pleasant sunny weather with gorgeous scenery. The ensemble cast of Jon Voight, Burt Reynolds, Ronny Cox, Ned Beatty, Bill McKinney and author James Dickey rivaled the efforts of the exceptional crew in *The Godfather* (1972), filmed in the same year. In fact, *Deliverance* would have swept the Oscars in any other year. The stars were mostly unknowns when the movie was filmed. Jon Voight had a breakout performance in *Midnight Cowboy* (1969), but *Deliverance* established him as a leading man and bankable star. *Deliverance* was Burt Reynolds' finest performance of his career, bar none. Had he continued to land similar roles, he would have been declared the new Marlon Brando. *Deliverance* was Ronny Cox and Ned Beatty's introductory roles, and many people don't realize that Bill McKinney, who played the hillbilly rapist, was not an actual Georgia rube, and went on to star in several Clint Eastwood movies, including *The Outlaw Josey Wales* (1976).

Deliverance begins innocuously, with loads of Appalachian landscape and buddy humor. Reynolds is the lead actor in these early scenes. The boys are looking forward to a great adventure canoeing on a doomed wilderness river in north Georgia. It's sad that such an unforgettable and entertaining scene – the dueling banjos with Ronny Cox and a mentally challenged young local – has become an American legend for all the wrong reasons. Just hum the first six notes of their tune and everyone will gasp in horror while imagining backwoods sexual assault. A clash of culture occurs early on when Reynolds and Voight get lost trying to find the river. One of the hillbilly guides asks, "Where ya goin', city boy?" Burt answers, "We'll find it," and the second hillbilly retorts, "It ain't nuthin' but the biggest f---ing river in the state."

The first day of canoeing is fun and exciting, along with a typical night of camping and locker-room jokes. Then comes the second day. Everyone is tired, sore, bug-bitten and hungover. They want to get home and watch golf. Early in the day, the two canoes drift apart on a lazy section of river, and Voight and Beatty row to shore in order to wait. Quick – what are the four actors' movie names? Voight – Ed, Reynolds – Lewis, Cox – Drew, Beatty – Bobby.

In the next scene, Beatty deservedly should have won the Academy Award for Best Supporting Actor. He and Voight are assaulted by two freaky-looking backwoods creeps. You know they're in trouble when Voight's Ed asks, "Look, what is it you require of us?" and McKinney replies, "What we, uh, require is that you get your god-damn asses up in them woods."

The sexual assault is neither pretty nor sugarcoated. It is realistic and shocking and not for the squeamish. "Squeal like a pig" is probably the most memorable line from the film. Afterward, McKinney asks his friend, "What d'ya wanna do now?" and the answer is, "He got a purty mouth," referring to Voight.

Then Reynolds comes to the rescue and puts an arrow into the chest of McKinney. The other hayseed manages to escape. When the decision is made to bury the body and not report the incident to authorities, Cox's Drew protests and says, "It's the law." To which Burt answers, "Law? What law, Drew? Show me the law."

There is a frightening nighttime scene on a cliff where Voight demonstrates the finest acting skills without dialogue. The movie is absolutely horrifying and will stick with you for a long time. It's like slowly sinking into quicksand and being unable to claw your way out of the mire. When James Dickey, playing a local sheriff, says, "Don' you boys do nuthin' like this again. Don' you come back here," you'll never want to enter the woods again.

In the end, when the movie concludes with a grisly hand rising out of the new lake, you'll feel like you've become the haunting figure in Edvard Munch's painting *The Scream*.

GK

Twelve

Southern Hospitality

*"It is a sin against hospitality to open your
doors and darken your countenance."*
- Proverb

*"In the South there are no strangers,
just friends we haven't met."*
- Anonymous

I WRITE LETTERS. It's just what I do. I've written letters
to Ray Bradbury and Jimmy Buffett, and gotten responses
from both. I wrote a letter to the coach of my Florida Gator
football team when I saw his players who represent my
school acting like criminals on the football field. He called
me in my classroom. I wrote a letter to the governor of our
state, which turned into an article titled "If you're yelling
you're not listening." I asked him if it was possible for him
to not treat teachers like cheap hired hands... Governor
Scott did not get back to me on that. I also write corny love
letters to my wife on birthdays and anniversaries. Like I
said, it's what I do. I wasn't born a Southerner, but I'd like
to think I learned hospitality from my Chicago-born mom
and dad; part of that comes out in letters.

But there's one letter that I remember vividly even though I wrote it almost twenty-five years ago. Letters are important in the moment; they are pertinent, usually to time and place. This one took on new meaning to me when the friend to whom I wrote this letter told me just last month that he still had it. He was packing up his Crystal River, Florida house to escape a hurricane, and he came up with the letter. He just wanted to tell me that he still had it. He lost the house but the letter had made it to the storage garage. Here's the situation that caused me to write that letter, and then thanks to Jef (Yes – he is a one "F" Jef), the letter included.

Our sons grew up in Little League Baseball together and Jef, having been an incredible player himself, coached all of his sons' teams. He has three sons: Eric, Matt and Drew. At that time, his construction company was growing, and becoming successful. Bottom line, between coaching baseball and working to grow his business, he overworked himself. And at some point his body (and possibly his mind) simply gave out. When I heard that Jef had collapsed in the third bases coach's box, I wish I could say I was surprised, but of course I wasn't. So I wrote him a letter, because that's what I do.

Hi Jef,

When I heard what happened at Highlands the other night, it scared the hell out of me. I thought of you, obviously, but I also thought of Debbie and the boys. I'm sure I wasn't as scared as you were, but it got my attention. Here's a line from one of my favorite Jimmy Buffett songs: "I can't run at this pace very long." Think about that Jef, think about the pace you run at. At work all day, weekends too, you have to admit. Then most nights you change in the car and turn into Coach Dad. When does it stop? When do YOU stop? You "stopped" the other night in the third base box.

You and I live very different lives, I know. As a teacher I can leave (most of) my work at school. That's not a luxury you seem to have. I'm sure after you get home from practice or games, you and Debbie probably scarf down some form of dinner, get the boys their baths, and then do some paperwork for the business. I literally don't see when you CAN stop. And I guess that's what still frightens me, buddy. So to you, what WAS the other night? A wake-up call? Just an aberration? You ended up horizontal on the ground in front of your son. Something has to give.

Here's my point Jef. I have to believe that there are way more important things than Little League Baseball ahead in our lives. I understand how much that special baseball field means to us. I believe it will be a thread that holds all of us, parents and kids, together as we get older. But Debbie needs you. Eric and Matt and Drew need you. That business you're building needs you. Whatever it was that happened to you the other night is not part of any plan you've made. Time to find a way to slow down. Here are two Jimmy Buffett tapes I recorded for you. I know you're more of a country guy than a Buffett guy, but I guarantee this music will ease your blood pressure.

Be well, friend –
Todd

Jef was not and is not one of my best friends, but we obviously have shared experience. For all the anxiety it caused for so many different reasons, I don't think there is anything more special than a father/son relationship during their Little League years. We loved our boys, five of them between us, and simply wanted to spend as much time with them as we could. The take-away line from that long-ago letter I guess was the "there are more important things than Little League Baseball ahead in our lives" line. That thankfully has turned out to be true. Two of those boys are running the same company he worked so hard to build, and Jef and Debbie don't have to "run at that pace" any longer.

Words matter. In this case my words mattered. All these years later, to realize that it meant enough to Jef that he would've kept that letter blows me away. I'm even more glad that he doesn't have to run or work at that pace anymore. Because if he did, I might find myself having to write another letter. Because that's what I do.

TC

IT WAS FRIDAY AFTERNOON on November 2nd. Saturday was the first day of hunting season. Elaine and I got off work early and were going water skiing. Such is life in Florida.

On the drive out on SR 40, we were hit by a pounding thunderstorm. It never sprinkles in Florida. Rain comes in thick sheets with drops the size of marbles. Most cars pulled off the road to wait out the storm. I kept driving. SR 40 is considered the most dangerous two-lane highway in the state and it's not a good idea to sit on the side of the road with thirty feet visibility. But the rain lasted only twenty minutes, and by the time we parked at Wildcat Lake there was glorious sunshine.

Most people think Wildcat Lake is merely a swimming pond, not realizing that around a corner it opens up to a large spring-fed lake with only two cabins dotting its shore. Also, there is a secret water trail that leads into a wet prairie that is stunningly gorgeous and loaded with waterfowl.

We took turns skiing. Elaine has a charming habit of pinching her nose before she goes into the water. She never falls. Whenever she's had enough, she simply lets go of the towline and pinches her nose. Not me. I take spectacular plunges. My fellow author Todd Carstenn is a magnificent skier. He taught me a trick to veer into the shallow water lilies close to shore, where the water is glass, and turn by sending up a rooster-tail of water. When I tried it, I did three somersaults and came up in gator/snake-infested weeds. I swam out like I was Michael Phelps.

"You forgot the ski," Elaine said.

"What?"

"The ski is in the weeds."

Crap! I swam back in for the ski.

The sun was starting to set when we returned to the boat ramp. We planned to pull the boat out and have dinner at the Blackwater Inn on the St. Johns River in Astor, but the Jeep wouldn't start. I had left the headlights on after the thunderstorm. Dang it! No cell phone connection and Astor was five miles away.

I was about to start hitchhiking when Elaine said, "I saw a light on in one of the cabins on the lake. Maybe someone will give us a jump."

"Good idea."

We hopped back into the boat and sped across the lake. Sure enough, the lights were on in the first cabin. I pulled up to the dock. Three or four monster trucks with Rebel flags and gun racks were parked out front. I could see several burly-looking men in the dining room eating and drinking beer. It was getting darker.

"I don't like the looks of this," I said.

"Why not?"

"Those guys may not like me sneaking up on them."

Elaine scoffed. "Go on. It can't hurt to ask. All they can do is say no."

"They could shoot me for trespassing."

After all, this WAS the Ocala National Forest.

"You watch too many movies," Elaine said.

I didn't budge.

"I'll go up there," she volunteered.

"Alright alright alright," I said. "Hope they spell my name right in the newspaper."

I stomped on the dock trying to make noise.

"Hello?" I yelled.

"Go up to the porch and knock on the door."

I inched forward. This plan was all wrong. Surprising a half-dozen armed rednecks that were drinking beer was not a wise idea, especially with Florida having a "Stand Your Ground" gun law. They could shoot me for sport and later claim I was creeping around and trying to break into the cabin – and every gun nut in the state would cheer.

I make plans and God laughs.

"Go on," Elaine said again.

I knocked on the glass in the door. All conversation inside the cabin ceased. I felt like the stranger in a cowboy movie who walks into a saloon and the music stops. The door creaked open.

"Hello," I said. "Sorry to bother you, but I'm at the boat ramp and my car won't start. I left the headlights on. Would anyone consider driving over to give me a jump?"

It was quiet and nobody smiled. Then suddenly it was Mardi Gras.

"No problem, dude," the guy at the door said with a huge grin. He shook my hand. "I'll be over there in five minutes."

One of the other guys said, "I wanna come."

When we got back across the lake, two monster trucks were already parked next to the Jeep and one had its hood up.

"I appreciate this so much," I said.

"I can't count the number of times I've done the same thing," the guy with the jumper cables said.

After the car was started and boat hooked up, they insisted we come back to the cabin for ribs and beer. First, however, I drove to Astor and bought two cases of Budweiser.

"I think you've made some new friends," Elaine said.

I smiled and nodded.

GK

Thirteen

Pure Water

"When a country wants television more than it wants clean water, they've lost their grip."
- Lewis Black

"Water is life, and clean water means health."
- Audrey Hepburn

THERE ARE THIRTY-TWO golf courses in Marion County, Florida. This county where I have lived for thirty-five years is not spectacular; it isn't a tourist destination, and while we do have lakes and rivers, we are land-locked. My point is that if a rural county like Marion, has almost three dozen golf courses, what do you think the number is for our ocean or gulf-access counties? Rhetorical question. But there's not much to debate. We have way more golf courses than our aquifer can handle. Let's see...clean drinking water for all, which comes as close to an inalienable right as we have, OR "Hey turn the sprinklers on, the sixth green has patches of brown, and the members won't like it." Are we capable of making decisions now that will affect all of us in the near and distant future? This is NOT a rhetorical question. It is one that demands thoughtful consideration. I am, however, a bit doubtful that thoughtfulness and consideration are possible anymore.

We also have a cattle rancher who has bought massive acreage in our vicinity. He requested the right to use thirteen million gallons of water per day for his business. That number is the equivalent of the number of gallons the entire county uses daily. He ended up "settling" for a little less than half of that, but up for discussion here is not necessarily his arrogance, but the thought that anyone could approach a governmental agency and request a usage permit equal to what the entire population needs.

That is mind-blowing. Is water so lightly considered, so blithely second-thought-ish, that someone could even contemplate that request? Here's your hint. No. Not in Florida, where, as I speak it hasn't rained in a month. The water shortage is real. We must, we rational thinkers, we must at least consider what life would be like without it. Dramatic? Hyperbolic? Maybe. But not by much.

And finally this.

In one of my classes I teach a poem called "Blessing" by the Pakistan-born poet Imtiaz Dharker. Without getting too much into the weeds with technical literary analysis, the poem is about a small village in extreme drought. One day, the municipal water pipe breaks and for a few glorious but frantic moments there is water – clean, fresh, rare, valuable-as-any-precious-metal water. For this village, Dharavi, outside of Bombay, India, this "accident," this pipe breaking IS a blessing, but amidst the joy of trying to capture this life-sustainer in buckets and containers of all kinds, one sobering fact is easily lost: it is a failure of a man-made pipe that bestows this blessing on the villagers. The drought is not over. There will be no change in their lives. The municipality will repair the pipe and it will be just as it was mere hours earlier...bone, dirt, dry. Whereas the burst pipe led to "naked children / screaming in the liquid sun," things will return to normal, where "skin cracks like a pod / there never is enough water." And so it goes.

I have thirty-two well-watered and manicured golf courses to choose from that are in my proverbial backyard. Our cattle rancher friend exaggerates his need for our water, but still gets half of what the whole area uses. A world away, real human beings in a remote village feel the actual tactile pain of the result of no rain. To say that we have a complicated relationship with Mother Nature and how much sustenance She can provide us is an understatement. But when we are all waiting on a day for a municipal pipe to break so we too can bathe momentarily in its "liquid sun"...that will be the day we fully understand that "water is life, and clean water means health."

TC

ELAINE AND I were driving up U.S. 53 in northern Minnesota on our way to Ash River. Ash River leads into Namakan Lake. On Cemetery Island in Namakan Lake was an old Ojibwa cemetery that was rumored to be haunted.

Ash River and Namakan Lake were also located within the boundaries of Voyageur National Park, established in 1975. A voyageur was a French-Canadian fur trader who plied the waters of the area in a canoe, circa 1700. Voyageurs cultivated excellent relations with Native American tribes, which was a unique twist for Europeans.

107

As we turned onto Highway 129 and entered the park, Elaine said, "Look at that."

I looked and saw a huge green and yellow statue of a walleye with a seat on its back so tourists could have their pictures taken while sitting on top.

I glanced at Elaine. "No way am I having my picture taken on top of that ridiculous thing."

"Don't be a party pooper," she said.

Voyageur National Park has lakes, rivers and thousands of islands. It has moose, black bears, timber wolves, white-tailed deer, foxes, weasels and river otters. Bald Eagles and loons, with their mournful cries, soar across the landscape. The northern section of the park borders Canada. The park consists of a boreal forest with large swaths of red and white pine, spruce, fir and numerous hardwoods including aspen, birch and maple. Most of the land surface in Voyageur is accessible only by water.

We arrived at Ash River Resort. An old codger walked with us out to the dock and rental boats.

"Normally I let boaters stay out 'til seven p.m.," the old codger said, "but today I need you back by five."

"How come?"

"My new girlfriend's taking me out for dinner in International Falls to celebrate our one month anniversary."

I tilted my head. The old boy had to be in his mid-eighties. It was 10:00 a.m. "We'll be back by four p.m.," I promised.

"Where ya goin'?"

"We'll cruise around and soak up the park. Then I want to explore Cemetery Island. My grandfather's best friend is supposed to be buried in the old Ojibwa graveyard. Is it easy to find?"

The old dude shuddered. "It's the third island once you enter Namakan Lake, and it has a sign. I used to take tourists out there, but ever since my old girlfriend took me to see *The Blair Witch Project*, I never went back. That place is haunted by shamans. If I were you, I'd skip it."

I looked at him with a grin. He was trying to spook me.

"Yeah, right," I said.

Ash River was lovely, but had too many fishermen. Once we reached Namakan Lake, however, it was like being a voyageur in 1700. The lake was a giant mirror. We spotted two bears on the shore of a small island.

"How'd they get there?" Elaine asked.

"That would be too weird to see a bear swimming in the middle of the lake."

I cut off the motor and we drifted. The water was sky blue, just like the ads for Hamm's Beer – the land of sky blue waters. I gazed into the water and could see twelve to fifteen feet down. I thought about the near lifeless lakes in upper New York and New Hampshire destroyed by acid rain. What are we doing to our planet? Water – it's the source of life. Someone told me I could dip a cup into the lakes of Voyageur and drink without treating or filtering.

Elaine and I both took a sip. The water was delicious.

This is how all of our lakes should be. Can you imagine being able to drink the water from the lake closest to your home with no ill effects?

Elaine pointed to the sign for Cemetery Island and we tied up to a birch. We searched the cemetery, but I couldn't find my grandfather's friend. His name was Arthur Bear Killer. The cemetery was serene and beautiful – if that's a proper term for it. It was 2:00 p.m. I built a small fire and planned to leave by 3:00 p.m.

I woke up at 4:15 p.m.

"Holy crap," I yowled. "The old dude is going to freak out and send the cavalry."

Elaine yawned. "What happened?"

I hit the gas and made it back to Ash River Resort by 5:10 p.m. The old codger was waiting on the dock with a scowl on his face.

"I almost had to send out the Indian guides," he said. "They're the only ones who'll go to Cemetery Island in the late afternoon."

"I'm sorry," I said. "I started a fire on the island at two p.m., and the next thing I knew it was after four."

"I told you not to go out there."

"Please – that place isn't haunted."

"Really?" He appeared bemused. "How many times have you fallen asleep on the ground with your head on a log for two hours? The shamans put a spell on you."

I thought about it. "You may have a point."

"I just got a chill up my back," Elaine said.

At the big walleye statue, I pulled over and asked a tourist from Arizona to take our picture on top.

"I can party with the best of 'em," I said to Elaine.

GK

Fourteen

Music

"And those who were seen dancing were thought to be insane by those who could not hear the music."

- Friedrich Nietzsche

"If I should ever die, God forbid, let this be my epitaph: THE ONLY PROOF HE NEEDED FOR THE EXISTENCE Of GOD WAS MUSIC."

- Kurt Vonnegut

"For the music is your special friend, dance on fire as it intends, music is your only friend, until the end."

- The Doors

"Mother Mother Ocean, I have heard you call,
Wanted to sail upon your waters, since I was
three feet tall…"

Jimmy Buffett, "A Pirate Looks at Forty"

I CROSSED THE FLORIDA state line for the first time in the spring of 1977 and I was never the same. I know, I know. Hyperbole and memories go together…like that old saying about "the older I get, the better I was." But this is different. It must have been different because all these years later I still remember that moment and cherish what it meant to my life.

We blew right through that state line and made it all the way down to the keys. This is where the idea of Paradise comes in. Growing up in a Wisconsin family that just didn't have the money to travel much, there were places on the map that seemed so unreachable that they almost made my heart hurt. One was California; the other was Florida. I crossed California off my to-do list when I spent my sophomore year in college at San Diego State with a bunch of my Wisconsin friends. But California wasn't for me. It fell way short of the wonderland I had built up in my mind. I would find out why it wasn't for me later, in retrospect, after I had spent time in Florida. The answer is actually quite simple: California is Florida on speed, and I couldn't handle that speed and that rhythm. I realize the word "rhythm" is an odd way of describing a place to live but it isn't to those of us who live on this finger of land between the Gulf of Mexico and the Atlantic Ocean.

Ahhh, as is the case with all sorts of storytelling, I am getting ahead of myself. I will end this particular digression with a line from a Jimmy Buffett song: "I can't run at this pace very long." When I heard that sentiment in his song "Tryin' To Reason With Hurricane Season," I flashed back to the reason California wasn't for me. I couldn't run at that pace, and that's Reason number one that this Wisconsin boy ended up in paradise.

That Keys trip was forty years ago, and it will probably come as no surprise that exact daily memories are dim now. I remember the incredible heat, almost cloying, but I grew to realize that the heat too was part of that rhythm I spoke of. And part of this rhythm for literally the entire Florida chapter of my life has been the guy I just mentioned, Jimmy Buffett. I won't go into why and how music becomes such a part of our DNA. I'm sure there is a specific reason that includes chemicals being released, etc., etc. But that turns something magical into science and that is not why Jimmy Buffett music has been a part of my life since that warm day in 1977 that I made it to the place I had once thought unreachable.

There is a THEN part of this story, my move to Florida, and a NOW part of this story that I'd like to offer here. If I added all the in-between parts it would be an autobiography, but that isn't the purpose behind any of this. The THEN part begins with Buffett's song "Changes in Latitudes, Changes in Attitudes." I won't go into his discography, but this song had been released just a few months before my first Florida trip. As I've said before in this book, I don't believe things happen for a reason, but I DO believe timing is important, and I also believe being aware and being awake to what life offers us IS important. I was an unhappy college student, about to become a drop out; I just didn't know it yet. So what do I hear on the eight track heading south? "It's these changes in latitudes, changes in attitudes, nothing remains quite the same."

The escape from the sameness, the lure of something different, practically foreign is a palpable memory of that first trip. The latitude change was obvious. Though Florida was only one time zone away, the weather spoke of the tropics. And "little latitudes" as Buffett suggests in another song ("Everybody's Got a Cousin in Miami"). But it was the attitudes that struck me the most. Keep in mind that I had as part of my recent travels, California still in my short-term recall. Again, I understand the fallibility of memory, but the seemingly frenzied nature of the West Coast rhythm in stark contrast to the Keys calm that I was now experiencing…it was simply what I needed in my life. It wasn't only the song, obviously, but the whole idea of change, in attitude AND latitude, that allowed me evaluate what I had been doing. I was able to realize that I had been playing a role in the charade that was my college life from which I was now on break. The role of dutiful son, the role of what young people should be striving for in their early twenties. I was failing at both roles.

Too much you say? Too much impact of a simple song? Certainly we are all products of ALL of our experiences, I get that, but to deny that small moments in people's lives have life changing repercussions is ridiculous. That moment all those years ago, made me realize that I didn't have to "run at that pace" anymore. I have never regretted for a second my decision to trade in mukluks and hand warmers for sandal golf shoes and shorts in December.

And so to the NOW part of this, and this has its roots in one of Buffett's more recent songs called "Savannah Fare You Well." I've always assumed it was about him realizing his daughter was about to leave home and venture out on her own. But the one thing I've always loved about his music is that I am able to take my own meaning from it. I adapt some of what he says and make it my own. Isn't that what music is supposed to be? For example, he sings about sailing and flying his seaplane to exotic ports of call. I don't do either and I don't paint myself as some beach bum who lives with sand between his toes. But I do see meaning in his songs, and as we have gotten older, he and I, there are more real similarities that I would ever have guessed speeding into Florida in 1977. This song about his daughter is one of them.

His song speaks of the relationship between father and child:

> "It's such a fragile magic
> A puff of wind can break the spell,
> And all the golden threads are frail as
> spider webs
> Savannah fare you well."

This song came out two months after my own son Jared left home and moved 4,682 miles to Waimanalo, Hawaii. So it seems I had said a similar kind of fare-you-well to a child. The "fragile magic" of a father-son relationship, the "puff of wind" able to "break the spell" of all the years and all the love I had spent with him. When I realized what that song was about, I felt a pain and a hurt so intense that it buckled my knees. Fragile and frail. Every parent feels that pain as we know it is THEIR time for new latitudes and attitudes. That song defined yet another moment in my life – that's what music can do – it is certainly what Jimmy Buffett has done for me as his songs have been an essential sound track of my life.

They say that when we remember something, we don't remember the actual moment, that we remember only the memory of that moment. The implication I guess is that there is fallibility, a gauzy imperfection of our recollections. I am fine with that. I am not some witness recalling testimony from my own life. I have been living

115

my life, fallibly and imperfectly for sixty-two years now. That Wisconsin boy, though still deep inside me, has been replaced. All those springtimes ago, I made my first trip to paradise, and Jimmy Buffett happened to come along for the ride.

TC

ELAINE AND I DROVE to St. Petersburg Beach and parked at the Beachcomber Bay Motel. It was one of those beach inns of yore – a long strip of shabby-chic cabanas lined with huge palm trees and surrounded by towering plush resorts. It wouldn't be long before this little gem would be taxed out of business and plowed under for a new gleaming condo complex.

Tonight we were going to attend the Tampa Bay Rays baseball game against the New York Yankees at Tropicana Field. It was sold-out because of the New York fans that live in St. Petersburg. Yankees love their Yankees.

I went for a run on the beach.

"Hurry back," Elaine said. "I want a mojito before dinner."

The sand was soft and sugar white. I figured on a four-mile round trip if I ran to the point at Pass-a-Grille. It was a gorgeous late afternoon with a light breeze. The tiny surf lapped the shore.

The Don CeSar Hotel was in sight. Known as the Pink Palace, the stunning art-deco hotel opened at the height of the Gatsby-era in 1928 and played host to presidents (FDR and JFK), bohemians (F. Scott and Zelda Fitzgerald), gangsters (Al Capone) and celebrities too numerous to list.

Famous musicians too.

My favorite rock band, Led Zeppelin, played before 56,800 fans at Tampa Stadium in 1973 and stayed at the Don CeSar Hotel. *Rolling Stone* called Led the "heaviest band of all-time" and "as influential as the Beatles." They also had a reputation for excess and debauchery.

I stopped running in front of the hotel and decided to take a peek inside. Luckily, I had slipped on my Tampa Bay Rays long-sleeved t-shirt before my run, or the security guard would not have let me in. I walked past the pool and entered the back door to the Maritana Grille, with its dozens of sea aquariums, and sat at the empty bar.

The bartender put down a napkin and said, "Mojitos are half-priced."

Too bad Elaine wasn't with me, I thought. "Better just have a Coke," I said. "I still have to run to Pass-a-Grille."

He brought my drink. "It's pretty dead here in the summer."

I smiled. "I just wanted to come in because my favorite rock band, Led Zeppelin, supposedly trashed a couple of rooms back in 1973."

"Yeah, I know," he said. "I was here."

I was agape. "Shut up! That was thirty years ago."

He smiled. "I've worked here for thirty-four years. I served them drinks."

"What'd they have?"

"You kidding? Jimmy Page made Jack Daniel's the swig of choice among rebel rockers."

I paused, and fought it hard, but it was no use. "I'll take a shot of Jack Black."

"I'll join you."

He poured two healthy shots and we clinked glasses.

"To Led," he said.

"To Led."

"People don't realize that Led Zeppelin could play all types of music," he said. "Heavy Metal – *Whole Lotta Love*, acoustics – *Gallows Pole*, soft rock – *Tangerine*, and of course incredible blues – *Since I've Been Loving You* and *When The Levee Breaks*."

"I saw them six times," I said, "and no matter how many encores they gave, the concert wasn't over until they played *Communication Breakdown*."

We had another shot of Jack Daniel's.

"I realize no one wants to hear it," I continued, "but unless you saw them live, you never truly experienced Led Zeppelin. They were an absolute stage band. Even film doesn't capture their incredible energy and presence. You had to feel the arena shake and rumble with Robert Plant wailing out the high notes while shaking his hair and tambourine, and Jimmy Page strumming or whacking his double-necked guitar with a violin bow, and John Bonham pounding the drums and going – well – bonzo. Nobody ever sat down at a Led Zeppelin concert. My friends and I would walk back to our cars from the L.A. Forum, and much of the conversation went something like this, "Wow, that was bitchin!'" – "What??!"

"I'll tell you," the bartender swore, "when those guys strutted through the lobby, you just knew that was how rock stars were supposed to look and act."

We had one more for the road.

I left the bar and stood on the beach. Pass-a-Grille was still a mile away. Crap – I couldn't run anymore. I had too many rebel rocker swigs of Jack Black.

I walked back to the Beachcomber Bay Motel.

GK

Fifteen

Rivers

"The river is everywhere."
> \- Herman Hesse

"Life is like a river, sometimes it sweeps you gently along and sometimes the rapids come out of nowhere."
> \- Emma Smith

"I've known rivers ancient as the world and older than the flow of human blood in human veins."
> \- Langston Hughes

"I THOUGHT HOW LOVELY and how strange a river is. It's always changing and is always on the move. And over time, the river itself changes too. Are people like that? I wondered. Am I like that?" (Aiden Chambers)

Isn't it strange to observe something that is always the same while in a constant state of flux? When we go camping in the Great Smoky Mountains National Park, in Tennessee or North Carolina, we inevitably search for a clearing or campsite next to water. Moving water. Most of the time this moving water isn't a river yet. It is a mountain stream that will turn into a creek that will find a river, eventually. One of my favorite things to do is to climb rocks upstream for as long as nature allows.

I sometimes wonder what I'm looking for; the natural beauty of all that surrounds me and the awesome strength and form of the boulders on which I climb are impressive. But it is the actual water that draws me on, ever more upstream. The way it puddles into tiny ponds over small rock faces. The way it forms ten-foot-deep pools over larger falls. I once found a huge freezing cold one which I immediately dubbed Todd's Pool, a dozen yards away from our tents. Of course the water doesn't stay in that pool for long. It is displaced by more and more flowing water, and so I continue my search and I climb more rocks.

Far better writers than I have described the magic in and of moving water. You look at one spot and all you see is that one spot. The reality is that one spot is different every second. The water moves, the river doesn't. That one moment is life in microcosm.

This might seem unrelated but bear with me. I looked down at my hands the other day and I saw my dad's hands. Years ago when I realized Dad was getting older (old?) it was his hands I noticed first. He was strong well into his seventies but in his late fifties it was his hands that gave it away. Thinner. A bit wrinkly. Age spots. How had that happened? I had looked at my dad my whole life, and he hadn't changed. Then I looked at his hands and those hands, those strong tan youthful hands that had thrown me high into the air at Merrill Hills pool so many summers ago...those hands were not what they had been.

How had THIS happened? I looked down at my own hands, the ones that had thrown my sons high into the air in any number of lakes or pools, all those summers ago...they hadn't changed at all. Until they had changed completely. Again in the words of Kurt Vonnegut: "So it goes."

So I repeat one last time: how did that all happen? Answer: the river happened. That moving body of water is constantly changing. I rock climb upstream in the mountains and I see the same stream but different water. I have been busy living my life and while I didn't see my hands change and become thinner and more wrinkly, they simply had. The river doesn't question its banks. I had not paid much attention to my hands; I have lived my life, not questioned it.

The river, every river, is lovely and strange, and changing. So too is life.

TC

I TOOK MY MOUNTAIN bike out to Sunnyhill Restoration Area. The area is made up of 4,505 acres of reclaimed muck farms on the banks of the Ocklawaha River. Sunnyhill has no trail signs; you just have to feel your way west toward the river. Unfortunately, this section of the river is a straight, dredged-out canal. The original bed of the Ocklawaha is on the property, and restoring the river to its natural course is the primary goal of the restoration area.

As loony as this idea sounds, in the 1930s the U.S. Army Corps of Engineers was authorized to construct a barge canal across the state of Florida, using several rivers including the Ocklawaha. The idiocy of the plan is beyond comprehension. Not only would the project ruin the rivers involved, it would also contaminate the Florida aquifer, which is an underground layer of porous limestone and rock that holds and filters the water that feeds our springs and lakes, and provides Floridians with their water supply.

From the late 1800s to the 1930s, before construction on the Cross Florida Barge Canal was begun, specially built paddleboats, extra tall and slender, plied the waters of the twisting river. Starting in Jacksonville, the paddleboats cruised up the St. Johns River, and entered the lower Ocklawaha in order to bring tourists to the headwaters of the fabulous Silver Springs. The boats traveled south while heading upriver since both the St. Johns and Ocklawaha run north, like the famous Nile River in North Africa.

North Florida joke:

Why does the St. Johns River flow north?

Because Georgia sucks!

Harriet Beecher Stowe, of *Uncle Tom's Cabin* fame, made the journey and called the wild and scenic voyage "a visit to fairyland."

As I pedaled along I kept an eye out for bear and moccasin snakes. I can almost guarantee you'll see bear and moccasin at Sunnyhill. The bear are good boys – they run away when they spot you. The moccasins are the thugs of the snake-world. They might attempt to strike as far away as seven feet. In comparison, rattlesnakes may strike within three feet. Moccasins are angry little suckers with no sense of humor.

I passed Ghost Pond – I think. I call it Ghost Pond because sometimes it's there and sometimes it's not. It's a superb location to watch a sunset. If the pond is gone, and there's only a dried indentation of grass, that means the ghost is on the move. On this trip, the ghost was gone.

I reached the long narrow ditch of a river. It stretched for five miles in either direction. It was sad to pass the original riverbed, but hopefully in the near future the original course will be restored. It was a cool and sunny day with a crisp breeze. I sat on the soft grass and enjoyed a beer. My eyelids grew heavy and I stretched out. In a blink of an eye I fell asleep. When I woke up, I stood and stretched. The air was moist and sweet – river air. I walked to the embankment and looked down at the shoreline.

Holy crap! A twelve-foot alligator was lounging not twenty feet away from the place I had napped. How long had that prehistoric monster been sitting there? I scooped up my pack and leaped onto the bike like I was Hopalong Cassidy. After about a hundred feet of furious pedaling, I looked back. No gator in pursuit, thank you.

GK

Sixteen

Mystery

"No, I would not want to live in a world without dragons, as I would not want to live in a world without magic, for that is a world without mystery, and that would be a world without faith."
                                          - R.A. Sanatore

"A world that might have Bigfoot and the Loch Ness Monster is clearly superior to one that definitely does not."
                                          - Chris Van Allsburg

TEACHING IS A transient profession. The statistics are a bit grim when it comes to the average length of a teaching career. A full 25% of us leave the classroom after only three years. I am blessed to have as friends at least a dozen teachers whom I have known for decades. They have helped me stay sane in this sometimes not-so-sane gig I have labored at for thirty-four years. Most of those who leave the classroom find employment in jobs like nursing or medical sales (huge money, I hear). I have also known some teachers who end up going to law school. Some sell insurance.

But I have a friend, I'll call him Jeff, who exchanged a high school classroom for the lecture hall of a university. I knew that when he decided to get his PhD that he was not long for our world. Sure enough, he got his doctorate and that was his ticket out.

I decided to write him a letter, partly because I truly do want to stay in touch with him, but mostly because I'm curious about the other world he now inhabits. This other world, while it doesn't have a Bigfoot or a Nessie, is simply a mystery to me. Probably because I could never see myself leaving this world, and the reality is that whatever he writes back will not clarify his leaving in the first place. I just can't fathom it.

Here is my letter to my former colleague.

Dear Jeff,

Since you left the sacred halls for a bigger, better (?), and higher level of Academia, not much has changed. Nevertheless, we must not forget our roots, must we Dr. University Professor? I know you haven't forgotten yours, but lest you need reminding, this is how my life is going.

After hall duty today on my way to a parent conference, I heard one of my colleagues screaming at a young couple to "stop groping each other in the hallway." I walked by the perpetrators with a hidden smile and a wink. They really hadn't been guilt of any mortal (moral?) crime; why then do they need to be screamed at? We older folk do forget what it was like to be young, don't we? Anyway, I had to get to my parent conference. The little yellow guidance reminder I held in my hand said that I was already ten minutes late. When was your last parent conference, Jeff?

How did the conference go, you ask? Let me tell you, my good doctor, it was one to remember. You recall the long brown wooden (are they real wood?) conference tables around which the teachers sit. The victim, the student I mean, sits at one end. The parent sits at the other. After eighteen minutes of hearing nothing but "late work," "bad attitude," and "low average," I broke in with, "but you ought to see his writing." I'm not sure how my fellow teachers and Steve's counselor did it, but they made me feel that this was neither the time nor the place for positive remarks. Steve was a slacker, damnit, and who was I to say that he wasn't. Later, I was able to learn from Steve's mom that my class was actually the only reason he was able to deal with the rest of the day. She shared that he had gone through some rough times and that he (and she) appreciated the freedom he was afforded in my class to be himself. His mom told me something before we both left the conference room: "He's really a good boy, Mr. Carstenn, it's just that…" I took hold of her arm and said I knew, no explanation was necessary.

Jeff, here's an excerpt from one of Steve's writings. This assignment had to do with a rite of passage. This is the kid with the late work, the bad attitude, and the low average.

"A man sang a beautiful song. Still no tears. It hadn't hit yet. Then it happened, they played a song called "Unchained Melody" by the Righteous Brothers. It was then that it finally registered. And then the minister began his sermon. When it was over, they wheeled the casket away."

Jeff, it went on for a few more pages, but you get the point, right? How do you help college kids deal with death, Jeff? I don't think I have an answer for my high schoolers.

127

After I left Steve and his mom, I rushed out to tennis practice; yeah, I'm still varsity boys coach. I had thought my guys would be practicing serves; they weren't. They were trying to scrape sand and dried mud left on the courts from the PE classes. We don't have a broom or blower so my eleven players were using their towels and their racket covers to make the court safe for play. There is no money in the tennis budget for brooms because we just had to pay for new nets. The PE classes ruined our old ones with their inane "Dyno-Ball" game. I don't know much about it besides they play it with a volleyball on my tennis courts. Does the varsity tennis coach at your university have a broom I can borrow?

You know this new Advanced Placement class I have, I'm teaching most of these kids for the second time. I had them as sophomores, now again as seniors. Every teacher should be lucky enough to get these kids ONCE, let alone twice. They really have grown up into the young adults I'd hoped they would. There is something else though Jeff, that comes to mind as a result of getting to know these young folks so well. The last day of school this year will probably be the toughest day of my career. I met these kids as fifteen-year-old sophomores; now they are eighteen-year-old seniors. Saying goodbye to them will be like letting go of my own. Do you hug your students when they leave, Jeff?

Speaking of the AP English class, here is another example of Steve's writing. It is modeled after a passage from "Autobiography," by John Stuart Mill.

"I was fifteen – young and optimistic, but I suppose we all were at one time or another. Life was simple then, a parade to smile and applaud at as the games went by. Now and then a clown would gambol up to the sidewalk and pinch my cheek with mirth, but he always returned to the parade. He always went back.

"It seemed that life was just that way. Some smiling face would saunter out of the crowd, play a tune or dance a jig...and disappear. That's the way life was and it was the way life was supposed to be. The sun shone on my parade as I watched it pass by. Different faces passed quickly then faded to black. This was the way life was supposed to FEEL.

"Until one day I saw a face come from the parade and walk quietly to the edge of my sidewalk and draw a small child up into his arms and carry her out to a brightly colored float. And I watched as she became...became one of the faces, until I could no longer tell which one was hers. The greatest pain came from the fact that for all the time I spent waving from that sidewalk, I had never fathomed that there could be anything else. Like a boy that had never known sight I felt no loss, but show that boy the sun...

"So for the remainder of my days, I decided that my life could not really begin until I found a way into that marvelous parade. So I waited and I smiled and when the clowns came close I waved extra hard and smiled the best I could. But they never stopped. I kept on waving and smiling, laughing at myself for thinking that there was something besides the waving as the smiles went right on by. And I guess the worst part was knowing that I had been right all along, knowing that all the smiles and all the waves would get me nowhere."

My Master degree in education didn't have a component on how to deal with Steve's disillusionment.

Got any suggestions, Dr. Jeff? What do college counselors say to the "Steves" at your school?

All for now buddy. I go by your classroom every day on the way to lunch. The teacher in there now, I have never seen her stand on her desk or heard her singing "New York, New York." Do you stand on your desk in front of your graduate students? I knew you did. Ain't it great how some things never change?

Hang in there Dr. Jeff,

Todd

So there's my letter. I realize as I re-read it that it is much more about me than it is about my departed friend who now teaches in the higher realms of Academe. I don't really know the take-away from that realization. I do know that I love my job and I guess I wanted to let Jeff know what he left behind was not some version of junior varsity education. He left. I stayed.

I never heard back from Jeff.

TC

OCKLAWAHA PRAIRIE IS an absolute gem. In North Florida, a prairie is an expansive wet marsh. A bridge crosses the Ocklawaha River and on the other side is a covered observation platform with benches and magnificent views. Wildlife abounds. You may see deer, bear, bobcat, fox and a horde of wading birds. Hawks, osprey and bald eagle patrol the skies. The breeze coming off the prairie is refreshing and smells of river and swamp. The platform is a grand place to get some thinking done while enjoying an adult beverage.

On my most recent trip to Ocklawaha Prairie, I was relaxing at the platform with a cup of wine when an odd-looking young fellow with spiked hair and thick glasses joined me. It was nearly sunset and getting chilly. I was slightly annoyed by the intrusion, but gracious.

"Care for a cup of wine?" I asked.

"Sure," he said. "Thanks."

He was lugging an impressive leather briefcase slung over his shoulder. After a few sips of wine, he took out a writing pad and started to jot down notes. I gazed at the prairie and ignored him. He kept glancing in my direction, and I sensed he had something he wanted to share.

I finally broke down and asked, "What are you writing?"

He seized the opportunity and handed me a business card. It read, "James E. Lindsay – Bigfoot Researcher," and had an imprint of the famous 1966 Roger Patterson photo of the big hairy guy. He then proceeded to explain that he was investigating a recent Bigfoot sighting in the area.

"Here?" I said. "On the prairie?"

"Yep."

He related the tale of an elderly couple from Belleview (a town about ten miles away) who had spotted two Bigfoot a month earlier from the bridge. Their story was considered credible, not only because they were respected retired schoolteachers who went straight to the local police with their story, but also because they told nearly identical versions while separated and questioned thoroughly by police. Plus, they had no monetary or ulterior motives and wanted to remain anonymous.

James was examining the prairie at the exact time when the sighting had occurred and was later going to meet the couple in Belleview for an interview.

I grinned at him. "What do you think really happened?"

He put on a stone face and informed me that there had been at least twelve credible sightings of Bigfoot in the Ocala National Forest, including a 1978 sighting by a Salt Springs Baptist minister. In fact, Seminole Indians spoke of a furry marauder prior to the 1835 Second Seminole Indian War and current forest dwellers often referred to the legend of a "skunk ape."

He said, "The Ocklawaha Prairie would make an ideal habitat for Bigfoot because of the many near-inaccessible sections."

I yawned. "I guess."

"I'm also investigating something far more intriguing. A woman named Denise Deschenes claims to have seen several Bigfoot in the Goethe State Forest just thirty miles from here and has photographed them. She said, 'I heard them walking with me. I know they're here.' She used the plural, them, indicating she believes there's more than one."

"When did this happen?"

"Two months ago. Deschenes still hikes out there and has developed an unusual ritual before her hikes that she believes draws the Bigfoot to her. Before entering the woods, she prays, waves, meditates and calls out 'Hello.'

She also leaves gift baskets containing crackers, tobacco and beef jerky."

When James mentioned beef jerky, I immediately thought about those silly commercials with a Bigfoot tossing juvenile pranksters into the air. I fought it hard, but couldn't restrain myself from bursting out with laughter.

"Dude," I chortled, "that lady's story is so lame."

He frowned. "You'll never be a believer."

"Sorry, James," I said. "Don't be mad."

He left in a huff. The sun had set and the swamp noises intensified. I was alone in an area where two adult Bigfoot had recently been spotted frolicking near the platform.

Bigfoot, I thought. Yeah, right.

I corked my wine and yelled, "Hey, James – wait up."

GK

Seventeen

Adventure

*"I wandered everywhere through cities
and countries wide.
And everywhere I went, the world
was on my side."*
                                    - Roman Payne

*"I know not all that may be coming, but be
it what it will, I'll go to it laughing."*
                                    - Herman Melville

ON A SPRING DAY thirty-five years ago, I didn't play tennis. I was supposed to, I had planned to, but I didn't. It turned out to be the best match I didn't play of my life. I had certainly been wandering, and in retrospect, what did and didn't happen that day, well, the world was definitely on my side. Adventure indeed.

I had been waiting for a half hour for my guy to show up. Tuscawilla Park has six courts, and at the far end, two guys were playing singles. All I could do was watch. After some time, they walked over to where I was sitting. I'm not a threatening guy, nor do I look all that creepy; I guess they were just curious. They asked me what I was doing, and I explained that my partner hadn't shown up. This conversation should have ended there; these two who I had never met before should've just gone back to their singles match – but they didn't. One of them simply asked: "What do you do in town?" My answer was that I was looking for an English teaching job, that I had just finished school and was in search of a classroom. Their response changed my life. They were teachers at a school called Lake Weir High and they would talk to their principal about any openings when they got back after spring break. My internal response was…"sure, sure you will," and I didn't give it another thought.

Which is why I was surprised when that same principal called me the next week. He said these exact words: "Lou and Gary told me their best friend was looking for a teaching job. Can you come see me later this week?" Yes. Yes, Mr. Folsom, principal of Lake Weir High School, I could to that.

I don't think things happen for a reason, mainly because I was never able to wrap my brain around a loving God hurting innocent people; I just couldn't work out the theology of that. But I do believe that when things DO happen, insightful, open, fortunate people take those opportunities, and run with them. If my tennis buddy had shown up that day. If Lou and Gary had decided to play earlier that day. (They HAD decided to play earlier that day but had to play later because of a problem at home.) If they were elementary school teachers. If there had been no openings for the fall of 1983. If Lou and Gary had not been curious about the guy sitting on the metal bleachers. If. If. If.

I worked with these two "best friends" for thirteen years, and along the way we became real best friends and I acquired more incredible buddies too, all at Lake Weir. I don't know if school colleagues are any different than insurance colleagues or colleagues who make widgets on the same assembly line. But these guys were first team...and then one day in 1995 Gary told us he was leaving to teach at another school. He ended up being just the first of us who exited to teach somewhere else. The buddy group started to disintegrate.

So this is what we did. We collectively decided that our friendships were worth too much to simply walk away, that since our planning periods were not the same anymore, because we were not going to eat the same crappy cafeteria food anymore, that we couldn't hang out. To that end, in that same fall of 1995, we began something we simply called Wings Night. Once a month, always on Thursday, we gather for beer and wings at a local dive called Charlie Horse. Past and present come together. We grew up teaching together and we are now growing old together, but we decided to keep track of each other along the way. There is not one of our group who even teaches at Lake Weir anymore, but for the last twenty-one years, we have not missed a month.

Certainly some of us miss an occasional Thursday. And life does get in the way. Our friend Bobby was killed in a car accident. Our friend Bill lost his wife to cancer. Some don't make it at all anymore.

But sometimes when one of our group can't make it to us, we make it to him. Howie has had some heart trouble in years past. He was a basketball coach for years, and a screamer, if you know what I mean. Not a referee's best friend. Anyway, one scheduled Wings Night, he was in the hospital. We smuggled beer and wings into his room. We all thought he'd hold off a bit on the amount of bleu cheese sauce he put on his wings that particular night, hospital bed-ridden as he was. Silly me. We didn't tell his wife.

1995 seems like yesterday. I'm sixty-one years old now. Gary has blown by sixty-five. Howie will be seventy soon. And yet we've acquired new blood along the way. Our sons come, and young teachers from area schools we've met at in-service trainings or what-have-you. These youngsters want to hang out with us, and drink beer and tell stories at Charlie Horse on monthly Thursday nights. Geez.

Years ago on a day I should have played tennis, I didn't. I've played hundreds of tennis matches since then, and they all sort of blend together. But that day is special for what I didn't do, and look what I gained in the process. Adventure? You could call it that.

TC

MY BROTHER CHRIS and I wanted to backpack up the Big Sur River to Barlow Flats and its magnificent gorge. We enlisted two friends to join us: Larry Larson and Craig. It was over three hundred miles up the coast, and since none of us possessed a car trustworthy enough to leave the Valley, we decided to hitchhike.

"Let's make it a contest," Larry said.

"Contest?"

"Race. Let's divide into teams and see which pair can make it to the trailhead first. Losers have to pack in the stoves and gas."

I glanced at Craig. "What are the teams?"

"You can't go with Chris," Craig said. "Brothers put out good karma on the road."

"Oh, bullshit!"

I looked at Craig again. He was huge with blond hair down to his waist. The year was 1970 and Charles Manson was still on the loose. We'd never get a ride.

When I mentioned Manson, Larry retold his story about meeting two Manson girls. "I picked them up in Topanga Canyon. They told me all about the ranch and Charlie."

"Really?" Chris said. "I met Zorro one night in Ralph's supermarket."

The four of us stood at the Balboa onramp to U.S. 101. A guy in a Jeep pulled over. I reached for the door handle, but Craig held my arm.

"Give 'em a head start," he said. "They'll need it."

I waved goodbye to Chris.

Minutes later, a vanload of surfers stopped and we climbed in and sat on their boards. They were heading to County Line Beach.

It's huge today, dude," one of them said. "Real gnarly."

They dropped us off at Decker Canyon and we sat for over an hour without seeing a car. Someone had written on a signpost: "This is a super place to contemplate life – no cars will bother you."

"We could die here," I said.

"Be positive, G," Craig said. "Look – here comes our ride."

A 396 SS Chevelle roared up and we hopped in. "Thank you for stopping," I said. "I didn't want to spend the night there."

"No problem," the neatly dressed and well-groomed man said. "The police are searching for a lone driver."

"What?"

Craig handed the driver a joint.

"Thanks," he said. "I hate reality."

We were dropped off in Carpinteria. Hundreds of teens hung out on the street corners in beach attire. Many gawked at Craig.

"We're only a few years older," Craig said, "yet they're acting like we're Martians."

A new Impala pulled up.

"I know you," the lady driver said. "G. Kent."

I looked. Holy cow! It was Georganne Alex. We went to school together for twelve years.

"Hey, G. A.," I said. "What are you doing here?"

"My husband and I own a boutique in Santa Barbara on State Street." She looked me over. "You need a haircut."

In Santa Barbara we noticed a wall of hitchhikers crowding the median of U.S. 101.

"Hitchhikers purgatory," Craig said.

"I'll drive you to UCSB in Isla Vista," Georganne said. "You'll have better luck."

A battered pickup pulled over. It was a Marine with a buzz haircut on leave. He reeked of Right Guard.

"I'd grow my hair if I could," he said, and laughed.

He took us to his mother's house in Nipomo and we sat on the back patio drinking Coors.

"Do you have some weed?" he asked.

Craig always had weed. He quickly rolled a joint. Once I witnessed Craig roll a joint on the back of a motorcycle doing forty miles per hour.

139

"Is your mom okay with it?" Craig asked.

"She'll smoke with us."

Sure enough, mom came out with sandwiches and more beer. She sat down and immediately began to bogart the joint.

"It's so boring around here," she said.

"Sure is pretty."

She looked around like it was the first time she ever noticed her yard. "I guess."

The Marine drove us back to U.S. 101.

Our final ride was a van with dogs and other hitchers. We got off at Pfeiffer Big Sur State Park. It was dark, and the crickets and frogs made a racket.

"Chris and Larry should be here," I said.

"We'll find 'em in the morning."

We set up camp by the river. Two other guys joined us. We smoked another joint and I warned them about the rangers.

"They'll come through camp real early to collect their fees. We gotta get up before them." Craig and I didn't have much money.

In the morning, Craig and I packed and then woke up the two dudes.

"You gotta move," Craig said.

"They won't come by this early," one said.

As soon as we walked into the trees, a ranger approached and collected ten dollars. Craig and I returned to make coffee after he left. The two dudes were mad at us.

"You owe us five dollars."

"Give me your address," Craig said. "I'll mail you a check."

At the trailhead to Barlow Flats and its famous gorge, we waited for Chris and Larry.

"I told you we'd win," Craig said. "You thought I'd be a handicap."

"Guilty as charged," I admitted, "only now we'll still have to pack in the stoves and gas."

GK

Eighteen

Ocean

"Hark, now hear the sailors cry
Smell the sea, and feel the sky
Let your soul and spirit fly into the mystic"
 - Van Morrison

"Your heart is like the ocean,
mysterious and dark."
 - Bob Dylan

I WAS IN THE WATER for maybe ten minutes before I was stung by jelly fish. Many jellyfish. A land-locked nineteen-year-old Wisconsinite and excited to be going to school in California. This was literally the first time I had set foot in salt water. The dreamy vision of those California beaches driven by the songs of the Beach Boys disappeared and was replaced by angry welts and painful itching. Welcome to California – don't let the door hit you on the ass on your way out.

This essay is to be about the ocean, or maybe oceans, or more accurately about beaches...since I don't have a boat. I will tell you though, for a Wisconsin boy, the California girls the Beach Boys sang about were real, at least in my dreams. Snow from November well into March and April. Lakes not really swimmable until June because of being frozen solid all those months. Snow drifts not only blocking front doors but also garage doors. I would listen to my 45 RPM singles, songs about California Girls, and California Dreamin' and Surfin' Safari and Surfer Girl, and Endless Summer...you get the idea. California stopped being a real place long before I showed up to be stung by those damn jellyfish. It was a symbol, a metaphor, a concept of what "when ocean meets sand" is supposed to look like. Ironically, I didn't make it to the ocean much during my one year of school in California. The San Diego State campus, believe it or not, was well inland and I was a nerd without a car. There would be no songs written about me. But this is about way more than California. I feel like I won at least part of the battle because by the time I was twenty-three, I had moved to Florida and the ocean and the gulf and the beaches here became less gauzily dream-like and became a genuine part of my life.

There are beaches you read about in magazines and then there are the beaches you go to. Waikiki Beach, in Honolulu, is beautiful of course with its sunset catamaran cruises with a close-up view of its neighbor Diamond Head. Duke Kahanamoku's restaurant is also a tourist must-see. Jimmy Buffett memorialized it in a song called "Duke's on Sunday." But like I said, those are places in magazines. Staying in Hawaii, take Waimanalo for instance. There are no Jimmy Buffett songs about Waimanalo Bay or Beach. It is the beach equivalent of a public golf course. The beach connected to Waimanalo Bay is small and simple and for both of those reasons, stunning. Old sailboats are pulled up into real backyards. Leash-less dogs scamper and bark at the waves and each other. This was the first Hawaiian salt water I set foot in. It wasn't church but I worshipfully attended every sunrise for the eight days I was there.

Closer to home, my home that is, is what I have heard is the World's Most Famous Beach, Daytona Beach. It is famous for Bike Week, guys turning left for 500 miles, and, like the Kardashians, it is also famous for merely being famous. Just north of Daytona, though, is Ormond Beach. This is another example of the difference between places you read about and places that touch your heart. Twenty-five years ago my sons and I made frequent summer trips to Ormond Beach. The boys would skim board, try to surf, and boogie board. When they started getting older, I was told not to call them "boogie boards." I was to call them "body boards." I never understood why. I didn't do much on these three-boy trips. I body surfed a bit, and I read. Nerdy English teacher reading at the beach? Present and accounted for. On occasion we would stay the night at a cheap little motel called Aqua Terrace, which was actually on the ocean, but with cracking walls, a pool in disrepair, and sketchy neighbors. But we were able to go to bed knowing we would wake up and still be at the beach. The places you go not the places you read about are what matter long term. Kenny Chesney has a song about memories called "I Go Back." To this day, when we drive by the old Aqua Terrace in Ormond Beach...well, I go back.

Finally, I've never been to South Beach, the Miami locale, home of all the glitterati and glamorous. Nobu, the sushi bar is there. DASH (Yes, all CAPS, it must be good), the Kardashian's boutique for "confident, captivating, and confident women of today, with an eye for fashion..." is also there. Ugh. The ocean part of South Beach, the beach part has been relegated to after-thought status. The pictures are stunning but they reveal a part of the salt, sand, and sea life that has nothing for me.

There is, however, a place a few hours north on the southwest Florida coast that does have my heart. It is the ocean that lures us, but it is the beach that provides our view. Palm Island is a small finger of sand near Englewood. You have to take a short ferry ride from the mainland to the island, and once you get to Palm Island resort your car stays parked. No driving. A few golf carts to get you down island to Stumps Pass for sunset every night. And lots of walking. What separates Palm Island from the rat race and the busy-ness of a place like South Beach (or Waikiki or Daytona et al) is the solitude. Mary and I took a walk one morning and we walked for almost an hour and we DIDN'T SEE ANYONE. I hike and camp because of the remoteness of it all; it is a form of pushing "pause" on the pace of life. Beach time does the same thing for me. I understand that up the beach an hour in Sarasota, or down the beach four hours to Miami, there are thousands of people elbowing each other out of the way for a towel-sized plot of sand. Not here. The beach, any beach really, as a destination, is nice. A secluded beach where you can hear small waves lapping as they meet the shore? Magical.

As a guy who grew up so many miles from anything salt-water related, I have made up for it with endless beach trips in the last forty years. There is danger of course of allowing them all to run together, to turn them into one rather bland re-run of each other. But maybe it's because I didn't grow up here that I have never allowed that to happen.

145

A simple and memorable moment happened on our first anniversary eight years ago, at Palm Island. Mary had suggested that we wear the clothes we were married in down to the beach, and have dinner. On the beach. With lawn chairs. And people walking by. I knew it was a bad idea from the start, and so of course we did it.

And it was wonderful. We took all of our stuff down to the foot of the Gulf of Mexico. Lo and behold fifty feet away there was a tent set up, under which a group of 50-something ladies were enjoying a get-away weekend. They saw us, as they walked a bit sideways at times, and had to tell us how romantic our idea (Mary's idea) was. They insisted on taking a picture of us, with the blue of the ocean and the white of the breaking waves behind us. I was sure it was going to be the corniest picture in the world. And it is. And it is my very favorite picture of the two of us. That picture simply doesn't work anywhere else. The canvas of water and sand, the sound track of waves and wind. I've used it before, but really only one word fits: magical.

I get the whole mysterious and dark aspect of the ocean, but for me it's always been something different. I have scuba dived (dove?) a couple hundred feet down into the cavernous darkness. I've seen some sea creatures from far away that I couldn't tell if they were friend or foe. But ironically it isn't down there that the ocean touches me. It is where the land meets sea that I feel most at home, I guess. That makes me what my friend Jimmy Buffett calls a mere "beach head sailor." For a Wisconsin boy who thought he might never even see the ocean, that is plenty good enough.

TC

THE MOMENT I STEPPED out of my car I knew it was going to be a special day. I had parked on the street and put coins in the meter; then I saw it. A monster wave lipped the top of the Huntington Beach pier and doused a crowd that was watching the surfers. My heart paused – the wave was at least eighteen feet!

It was cold. I left my leather coat in the car, but kept the fleece. After unstrapping my surfboard from the racks, I walked across the sand and found a group of surfers who had "circled the wagons." That meant they had formed a perimeter with surfboards that created a safe zone for clothes and other valuables. Unfortunately, surfers and beachcombers are the biggest thieves on the planet. In a safe zone, at least two surfers remained to guard at all times. Six surfers sat within the circle.

"Mind if I join you?" I asked. I wasn't a local, so proper decorum was expected. Never assume you'll be welcome.

"Sure," one said. "You paddling out?"

I glanced at the line-up. Only about ten surfers sat near the takeoff point, and most kept their distance from the pier. Another crusher curled under the pier and smashed among the pilings with no one riding it.

"I may try it."

A second surfer looked at me. "Aren't you friends with Larry Larson? I've seen you two together. He's out in the water."

Larry Larson was the most well-known and spectacular surfer from the San Fernando Valley. People always recognized him by his two long black braids that flew in the wind while he rode a wave. We had gone to junior high school together and started surfing at the age of thirteen.

I stood in knee-deep water, clad in a full wetsuit, and waxed my board. Then I rubbed a handful of sand into the coating. Several lines of four-foot-high soup rumbled to shore. Paddling out was going to be a challenge. I had surfed Rincon, and Makaha in Hawaii, at ten to twelve feet, but nothing like this. These walls were fifteen to twenty feet and thick as semi-trucks.

A handful of local kids with long blond hair stood in the shallows hoping to save a board from the pier pilings for a tip. This was before leashes, and if you lost your board it bounced all the way to shore and you had to swim.

Huntington Beach looked like it was holding a surf contest. Several vans with the *Surfer Magazine* logo were parked in the sand. Photographers jammed the beach with an array of cameras while a mass of surfer girls stood on the pier wearing tight jeans and boots. A car stereo played "Good Vibrations" by the Beach Boys.

I paddled up next to Larson and then sat on my board. "How is it?" I asked.

"The lefts are gnarly," he said. "The rights have perfect form but close out next to the pier. If you go right, be sure to kick out quickly."

I looked at the other surfers waiting for the next set. "We're out of our territory." Larson and I were North Bay regulars.

"It's okay," he said. "They're good guys. They respect us for paddling out. Plus, I think they're scared."

Photographers on the pier yelled that a big swell was approaching. I held back on the first wave out of deference to the locals.

"Take it," Larson shouted.

"You sure?"

"Go, boy."

I started to paddle. As the wave lifted my board, spray hit me in the face. Dropping in quickly, I banked off the lip and was nearly eye-level with the surfer girls on the pier. It was a fifteen-foot drop. Surfers paddling out hooted. I kicked out next to the pier and immediately started to paddle back out. Once again, photographers pointed outside and yelled to me about another big one lipping the end of the pier. I watched the other surfers paddle up the wall and go over. I paddled harder. At the top of the wave, the crest curled and sent me backwards over the falls.

My board disappeared and I tumbled under water. I didn't know which way was up. The water turbulence bounced me around like a cork. I ran out of air and started to panic. Then, I just gave up. I opened my eyes to darkness and felt calmness. This must be how it feels to drown. Suddenly I broke the surface and gasped for air. No one on the pier had noticed my predicament. I could have drowned and no one would have known until my body washed ashore.

I figured my board was in pieces.

Then I saw him. A twelve-year-old with hair down to his shoulders stood in the soup with my board in his hands.

"Wow, kid – thanks." I was out of breath. He didn't hand me the board. Then I realized what he was waiting for.

"Follow me to the safe zone," I said. "My wallet's there."

GK

Nineteen

Culture

*"Preservation of one's own culture does
not require contempt and disrespect
for other cultures."*
- Cesar Chavez

*"A nation's culture resides in the hearts
and in the soul of the people."*
- Mahatma Gandhi

GOLF IS FLOG spelled backwards.

Golf is a solitary game. It is a one on one scenario,
you against the course. There are moments on the golf
course that border on spiritual because of that solitude.
Sunset on a golf course is a near-sacred time. Quietude.
Calm. Serenity. Peace. Then the darkness comes, and the
morning, and it all begins again.

Against the backdrop of all this existential beauty
though, is something called the Muni Golfer. On television,
we see the Masters at Augusta, the British Open at
Carnoustie or the Old Course. We see the Players
Championship at the Tournament Players Club in Ponte
Vedra. I would like to introduce another fragment of the
golfing population, a species that differs greatly from those

150

khaki-wearing flat bellies on tour: the aforementioned Muni Golfer, also known as the Muni Rat. "Muni" is derived from "municipal," which means "public." And "public" in golf terms almost always means "cheap." The bottom line is that we Muni Rats play public courses, not country clubs. Let me define what a Muni golf course is. It is the equivalent of a stepchild, it is Side B of the old 45 RPM singles, it's the movie that shows opposite the new Star Wars debut, it's the show ESPN airs opposite the Super Bowl. A Muni course is Shemp (the 4th Stooge), it's Frank Stallone, it's the drummer before Ringo, it's Garfunkel. It's the Pips, it's…it's, well, you get the idea.

The Muni Golfer is the human equivalent of the Muni golf course. We often wear tie-dye instead of collared shirts. We often don't tuck in our shirt, whatever type or style. We wear sandal golf shoes. We have offensive nicknames for the guys we play with. We get dressed in our cars and we drop trow in the parking lot. But even with all that, our Muni, to us, is Augusta in April. Being a Muni Rat doesn't necessarily make us better or worse than our country club brethren; it doesn't make us rich or poor, high handicap or low. It is simply who we are. The famous Popeye, who I believe played at a Muni just outside of Boston, had it right all along when he said, "I yam what I yam and that's all that I yam." That's us. We know what we am.

I can see that the implication of describing the kinds of golf courses and the kinds of golfers we are might be that we are, um…less than bright. And while it is true there are no MENSA members among us, there is one bit of proof that we actually are on an elevated plane of being. The proof? We have created our own language, our own culture, if you will. Does that mean that we are "cultured"? I'll let you be the judge of that. Yes, this jargon is specific just to us. "Jargon" has two definitions. It is the "specialized or technical language of a trade" or it is "nonsensical, meaningless, or incoherent talk." The "trade"? Golf, of course. Nonsense? Incoherent? You bet. Meaningless? That I disagree with, because to us it is all (the golf, the courses, the buddies) worth more than gold.

It is with this in mind that I initiate you, humble reader, into our Muni Rat society by sharing some of that specialized language. Some of the words, granted, are not new words, per se, but as you'll see, we have our own take on them.

BEER: Beer is one of the four food groups and we have our own names for each type of beer. In no particular order: CREAMY RED and BUD HEAVY both apply to regular Budweiser. A BLUE YUMMY is a Bud Light. A LADY FISH is the new white Miller Lite can. A BLUE FISH is the tall sixteen-ounce Busch can. Our muni charges the same for the BLUE FISH as it does for the twelve-ounce beers. That is four ounces for free. Muni Rats know bargains when we see them. What about Heineken or Guinness you ask? Did you forget whom we're talking about here?

F.I.D.O.: Golf, being an addiction, lures us in, and then steals our souls. A point is reached in each round of golf when we simply have no more to give. The Golf Gods have decided that this day will not be pleasant. We hit a ball in the sand trap and it lands in a deep foot print the idiots ahead of us did not rake. The beer cart girl mashes the gas pedal during our backswing and we shank the ball at an almost perfect 90-degree angle. We have a new sleeve of Titleist balls ($52 a dozen). We hit one in the street. We hit one in the pond. Energy sapped and motivation waning, we tell our buddy who is at the wheel…"Fuck It. Drive On."

JIGGULATED (also JIMMY JAMMED): The Official Muni Rat Golf Glossary defines this as "to become nervous, anxious, all tied up."

You are on the first tee of the monthly muni golf association event. It's early and it's wet and you are teeing off into a blinding rising sun. Add to that, your tee time is the first of the day, so everyone is watching you. You are so jiggulated by the confluence of these events that you almost whiff the ball entirely. You do manage to actually make contact and you look up in time to see it dribbling forward…and it stops right before it makes it to the ladies tee box. And of course as a Muni Rat you know what that means: you have to play the rest of that hole with your pants down. No really – it's in the handbook. Good luck with that, Sparky. Play well.

Related term: PREMATURE EJIGGULATION: the state of being nervous before you even get to the golf course.

BALL ME: Par three, 190 yards carry over water, dead into a gale force wind. Your normal ball flight is high, and on a day like this, that is unfortunate. You crush a three iron which immediately balloons up into the wind and it splashes painfully into the middle of the lake. Before the ball even hits the water though, you hold your hand out, ready to hit another shot and you say to your buddy, "Ball me," as he reaches into your bag for another Titleist. Attempt # 2. You use the same club expecting different results. Genius. Same results. "Ball me," you say yet again and your buddy obliges. Attempt # 3. You change clubs but are thinking instead of the money you're tossing into the water in the form of those golf balls. This attempt, though valiant, also finds the bottom of the lake. "Ball me." OK – stop saying that. Now you sound like a deviant.

STANK ON MY HANG-DOWN: Umm...never mind.

I will end with this.

Who do we spend as much time with as our wives or our girlfriends? Our therapist? Nope. Our co-workers? They wish. Our children? Probably should, but no. Our golf buddies? Right on, Sparky. There is a group of Muni Rats who can be found every weekday afternoon at the golf course. We don't all play every day but some fraction of us is always out there. So let me confirm the suspicions right here. Let's see...eight or ten guys who spend THAT much time together, speaking the same cute little golf lingo, telling the same stories over and over again, occasionally touching each other in that congratulatory way those kinds of special friends will. Yep, we are all – WHAT? What did you think I was going to say?

No. Here's the suspicion I want to confirm. We are all...golf buddies. And if you have golf buddies, you know what that means.

I simply don't know what I would do without these guys, this culture of the Muni Rat. They have every right to beat me senseless for all the ways I insult them. Since I'm the scribe of the group (for example, half of them won't know what "scribe" means) I'm the one who has revealed their shortcomings in numerous ways, both public and private, for years. But they don't. Because, well because we're golf buddies, and as long as we can stand up long enough to hit a shot I will continue to make that trip back to our muni.

TC

ELAINE, MY BROTHER CHRIS, his wife Liz and I hiked up a narrow trail to Boquillas Canyon lookout on the Rio Grande River in Big Bend National Park in Texas. It was about ten minutes until sunset. An elderly Hispanic gentleman – who resembled the ghost in Robert Redford's *The Milagro Beanfield War* – sat on a tiny bench at the point.

We stopped talking.

"Welcome," he said, "to the finest vista in all Mexico."

I smiled. "I believe we're in Texas."

He shrugged. "Are we? At one time this was all Mexico."

"Where do you live?" Chris asked.

He pointed south. "Boquillas del Carmen. See the lights?" About a dozen lights twinkled in the desert. "I cross the river every afternoon to watch the sunset."

There was no bridge. "How do you get across the river?"

He held up his hand. *"Tiempo de la puesta del sol –* sunset time. Wanna make a bet?"

I tilted my head. "Bet?"

"I'll bet we see the green flash tonight," he said.

155

When conditions are right, a green flash is visible just above the upper rim of the sun as it sinks below the horizon. It usually lasts no more than a second or two.

"That's a myth," I said.

Elaine added, "I think it only happens over water."

The old gentleman persisted. "Wanna bet?"

"I'll bet," Chris said. "What's our wager?"

"If I win you buy me a quart of rocky road ice cream. I love rocky road. If you win I'll give you an old and very valuable Mexican gold coin."

"I'll have to go to the camp store for the rocky road," Chris said.

"My gold coin is in Boquillas del Carmen."

"How do we settle up?"

He thought for a moment. "Come to Boquillas tomorrow and meet me at the fountain. Be sure to bring my rocky road. There's no ice cream in town."

"I can pack it in the little ice chest," Chris said, "but I'm not gonna lose."

"Hush," *El Viejo* said. "Sun is going down."

Poof – a green flash was clearly visible.

"Son of a gun," I said. "I've never seen it before."

The old man grinned and started to walk down the trail. "See you *mañana* in Boquillas."

"Wait," Chris said. "How do we get there?"

He pointed south again. "Go to the river bend. You'll find your way."

At noon the next day we stood by the river bend with a little ice chest containing two quarts of rocky road ice cream. A man sat in a rowboat on the other side of the river.

"What do you think?" Chris asked.

I waved and the man rowed to our side.

"Two dollars each, round trip," he said. We paid up.

On the other side of the river another man stood next to a corral with about a dozen burros.

"Three dollars each, round trip," he said.

"To Boquillas del Carmen?" I asked.

"Nowhere else to go."

The burros were hobbled, which made us bounce even more when they attempted to trot. Three horsemen rode out of the brush and blocked our path. I didn't feel so tough riding a burro.

"Kilos?" one asked.

"He wants us to buy marijuana," Liz said.

"*Gracias*, no."

They shrugged and rode off.

In the tiny town of Boquillas del Carmen, several little rascals herded our burros to a hitching post with switches and tied them up. I paid them each a quarter. A fountain sat in the center of the plaza. The girls headed for a small shop with handmade jewelry. Chris and I sat at an outdoor café and ordered Tecate. The elderly gentleman was nowhere in sight.

The bartender pointed to our ice chest. "Rocky road?"

"Yep. How'd you know?"

"Leave it with me," he said. "My uncle regrets that he had a prior engagement."

I looked at Chris. "Okay."

He handed Chris a tiny box. "He also asked me to give you this."

Inside the box was a small Mexican gold coin.

I looked up. "We can't accept this. We lost a bet."

"It would be considered impolite to refuse his gift," the bartender said.

Chris put the tiny box in his pocket. "Please tell your uncle *muchas gracias*."

The bartender bowed.

"*El baño, por favor?*" I asked.

He pointed to the back of the building. We walked to where he had pointed and looked around.

"There's no bathroom back here," I said.

We stood next to a gully. Chris peered over the side and said, "Look."

Lines of toilet paper, stuck to the cacti and brush, rippled in the breeze.

"This IS the bathroom," he said.

We choked with laughter – and peed into the gully.

"Different culture," Chris said with a smile. "A very different culture."

GK

Twenty

God

"God will not look you over for medals, degrees or riches, but for scars."
                                        - Elbert Hubbard

"Life is a journey toward God, and no one has the right to insist that you go a certain road."
                                        - Pat Buckley

"I think God gave every one of us a cellphone. We just dropped it."
                                        - Sylvia Browne

"EVERYTHING HAPPENS for a reason."

No. No it doesn't.

This sentiment is often used as a response when something in a person's life has gone wrong. But if it's the response on a personal level, why wouldn't it also be so on a local or national level or even on a world scale? This is where God comes in. My response to the "everything happens for a reason" mantra is that I cannot fathom a loving God doing awful things so we could...so we could what? So we could see the error of our ways?

September 11, 2001. Hurricane Katrina. The Rwandan Genocide. The Pulse Nightclub massacre. Sandy Hook.

The Holocaust. Losing a granddaughter before she was born.

Things happen for a reason.

No. No they don't.

But this is what I DO know. I believe that we, collectively and individually, are somehow able to process what has befallen us and from that point, we carry on. We are not God's pawns whom he puts through the paces. I'm not saying that God is not part of the process; He is. It is after it (whatever disaster, large or small) all falls down that we need Him the most. And this is where the idea of the cell phone comes in.

The connection between God and me is strong when I am in church listening to my Mary in her string choir playing her violin for the congregation on quiet Sunday mornings. I hear and feel God clearly on those too-rare times that I have both of my sons within hugging distance of me. He is there on my solo hikes, and His voice is as much the birds and the breeze and the lapping water as it is the soundless stillness.

I love God and believe strongly in His grace but I've dropped that phone way too often in my life. What did I think I was accomplishing in the mid 70's? What was I doing to myself and my family? I wasn't listening. What good is it to be afraid on a daily basis about things over which I have no control? I'm not listening. Of what possible use is it to allow the inane discord of our politics to make me applaud someone's failure at the expense of our country? I'm listening, but not to the right Voice.

I fail at a lot of things, I have fumbled that phone too much in my life, but to His credit, I am able to move on. And these are some of the things I see when I do. I see my

Mary with her head bowed, first thing in the morning, going over her prayer list. I see our grandson, born to a daughter we were relatively sure would never have a child. I remember thirty-four years' worth of students who have helped to make me whole. I see friends with whom I am growing old. I hold in my heart a mom and a dad and a brother I miss more than you could ever know. But they are in my heart and my soul and my memory, and it is because, to continue this metaphor, I have picked up the phone again, that I am where I am in my life.

I used to get a bit wiggly when the subject of God came up. I have known Mary fifteen years now and I credit her for helping to make God a more daily and permanent part of me. And so at this stage of my life, it is with sincerity that I say, using the words of my favorite Christian…"I'm not who I was."

And the Voice at the other end of the line says, "Amen."

TC

ELAINE AND I DROVE to the Acoma Pueblo, aptly nicknamed Sky City or Pueblo in the Sky. When you see it, you'll know why. We drove sixty miles west of Albuquerque and then twenty miles south of Casa Blanca. The Acoma reservation has 500,000 acres, about one-tenth of its historic lands. In the 2010 census, 4,989 people were identified as Acoma. That's quite a tiny minority. The Acoma people have continuously occupied Sky City for over eight hundred years, making it one of the oldest inhabited communities in North America. The mesa is 365 feet tall. Acoma traditions, including their native religion, have been practiced for two thousand years.

Acoma means "place that always was."

I parked in a dirt lot next to a sign that read: Wait Here. No other cars were in sight. Elaine spotted the vertical staircase that historically was the only access to the pueblo and easily defendable. Today, a narrow dirt road winds to the top. We leaned against the van and waited – and waited. Another car pulled up with a mom, dad and two teenage daughters.

Dad read the sign and smiled at us. "I guess someone will be down for us in a few minutes."

"We've waited for over an hour," Elaine said.

One of the teens pointed to the mesa. "Look."

We looked. A lone slender man with long braided hair strolled down the narrow dirt road. I could see he was very young.

"The pueblo is closed today," he announced. "We have a religious ceremony. But one of the elders saw you waiting and said, 'Let 'em come up.'"

Religious ceremonies are usually closed to the outside world, he explained. If we happened to catch a glimpse of what was going on during the tour, we must not speak or take pictures. We paid ten dollars each and began our trek up the road.

At the top of the mesa were over three hundred adobe buildings, some two and three stories high with ladders stretching to the upper floors. No electricity or running water. Cisterns were used to catch rainwater. The land surrounding the mesa was velvety green with wild grass and mesquite. Other mesas and tall mountains were in the far distance. Though Sky City was nearly impregnable to enemy tribes, it was no match for Spanish guns, cannons, swords and horses.

At the end of the road, a nice lady offered free soda or water, which we all took gratefully. Her table was next to an adobe oven and Acoma tacos were three dollars apiece. Once again, we all partook. Several other women sold pottery and jewelry. Elaine admired a simple piece of pottery with a hand-painted deer.

"Forty dollars," the elderly woman said.

"I can only afford thirty," I countered.

She smiled, but didn't answer. We started to walk away.

"Okay," she said. "Good deal."

The Catholic church was magnificent, especially the interior. When we got back outside, I asked our guide, "Where'd they get those beams?" The surrounding terrain was desert.

He pointed north. "See Mount Taylor?" The mountain was at least twenty-five miles away. I nodded. "The Spanish soldiers forced our men to carry the beams from there. It was a long and difficult journey."

Although we weren't allowed to attend the ceremony, at several intersections we could observe.

"Remember," our young guide reminded us, "do not speak or take pictures."

The ceremony appeared solemn, with a rhythmic drumbeat and shamans dressed in bright costumes. This was not some silly mumbo-jumbo ritual, but a serious and important ceremony stressing harmony between all life and nature. I thought about all the foolish movie portrayals of Native American rituals with crazed medicine men shouting gibberish about a Great Spirit in the sky – well, maybe that Great Spirit is God, the same God for Jews, Christians and Muslims. The Acoma people are not primitive or backward folk. Their systems of family, honor and justice are not inferior to ours. In fact, in many ways they're superior, and certainly lack the exclusiveness and hypocritical nature of other world societies and religions. Their religion was natural, relevant and thoughtful – and made perfect sense.

It's always amazed me to learn how people throughout the world and throughout time, independent of each other, have come up with the concept of an all-powerful force that must be God, the one true God. And since this idea of God is a feature that exists in all people, it must be innate, and therefore true.

Our group walked back down the winding narrow road to our cars carrying pottery and pieces of jewelry. I glanced back at Sky City and saw our teen guide watching us.

He waved.

GK

Epilogue

" 'Why did you do all this for me?' he asked. 'I
don't deserve it. I've never done anything for you.'
'You have been my friend,' replied Charlotte.
'That in itself is a tremendous thing.' "
                                        - E.B. White

"A friend is someone who knows
all about you and still loves you."
                                        - Elbert Hubbard

MY BUDDY TODD CARSTENN and I hiked along
Cataloochee Creek on our way out of Great Smoky
Mountains National Park. The year was 1994 and we were
wrapping up our annual summer backpacking trip.

It was a steamy afternoon. Following a mid-morning
downpour, the sun leaped out and was blazing. Our glasses
fogged up. The car was parked next to the most exquisite
meadow in the park. It had been used as a battlefield in the
1992 film *The Last of the Mohicans* starring Daniel Day-
Lewis, Madeleine Stowe, Russell Means and Wes Studi.
The car desperately needed gas and we desperately needed
beer. At the first convenience store, in Dellwood, signs in
the windows read: milk, bread and cigarettes. I sensed
disaster.

"I don't like the looks of this."

Sure enough, we were in a dry county. North Carolina
and Tennessee have plenty of them. The second store,
outside of Waterville, was also a bust.

"We still need gas," I said.

In Cosby, Todd pulled into a third store and went inside to pay while I pumped the gas. The store was one of those relics that allowed you to pump first and then pay. How refreshing! I sat back down in the passenger seat and sulked.

Suddenly, there was a knock on my window. I looked up. My very best friend Todd Carstenn stood next to the car with a huge grin on his face. In his arms, he carried a case of ice-cold Budweiser.

Recommended Reading

1. *Desert Solitaire,* Edward Abbey
2. *1984,* George Orwell
3. *Socrates Café,* Christopher Phillips
4. *Blue Highways,* William Least Heat Moon
5. *The Vintage Bradbury,* Ray Bradbury
6. *The Call of the Wild,* Jack London
7. *The Sunset Limited,* Cormac McCarthy
8. *Johnny Got His Gun,* Dalton Trumbo
9. *To Kill A Mockingbird,* Harper Lee
10. *The Monkey Wrench Gang,* Edward Abbey

Acknowledgements

The authors wish to thank Mary Carstenn, Jared Carstenn, Dustin Carstenn, E. Elizabeth Kent and Elaine Springer Kent for support and encouragement.

Thanks to Christopher Phillips for inspiration and *Socrates Café*.

Thank you Dan Barth for expert editing and book design.

Special thanks to Charlie Horse Restaurant where the idea for this book was conceived over many beers.

Front cover photo of Carney Island and back cover photo of Todd Carstenn and G. Kent at Barr Hammock by Rob Burgess.

About the Authors

Todd Carstenn used to copy favorite lines out of books and songs, and tape them to his bedroom wall. That he turned out to be an English teacher is no surprise. His love of the written word comes out in these often-philosophical reflections on what life has turned out to be.

G. Kent was born and raised in Los Angeles. He has lived in Ocala, Florida for over thirty years. He is also the author of *Granada Hills Blood* (Bandit Press, 2016) and *Bandits on the Rim* (Tenacity Press, 2012).

Made in the USA
Lexington, KY
09 July 2017